The Secret Language of Flowers

The Secret Language of Flowers

Liz Dobbs

Produced for DK by Toucan Books

DK LONDON
Senior Editor Scarlett O'Hara
Senior Designer Mark Cavanagh
Managing Editor Gareth Jones
Senior Managing Art Editor Lee Griffiths
Production Editor Jacqueline Street-Elkayam
Production Controller Nancy-Jane Maum
Illustrator Emma Fraser Reid
Jacket Design Development Manager
Sophia M.T.T.
Jacket Designer Akiko Kato
Associate Publishing Director Liz Wheeler
Art Director Karen Self
Publishing Director Jonathan Metcalf

DK DELHI
Senior DTP Designer: Harish Aggarwal
Senior Jackets Coordinator: Priyanka Sharma-Saddi

First published in Great Britain in 2022 by
Dorling Kindersley Limited
DK, One Embassy Gardens, 8 Viaduct Gardens,
London, SW11 7BW

The authorized representative in the EEA is
Dorling Kindersley Verlag GmbH. Arnulfstr. 124,
80636 Munich, Germany

Copyright © 2022 Dorling Kindersley Limited
A Penguin Random House Company
10 9 8 7 6 5 4 3 2
002–329232–Jan/2023

A CIP catalogue record for this book
is available from the British Library.
ISBN: 978-0-2415-6622-0

Printed and bound in China

For the curious
www.dk.com

Contents

Autumn

Winter

Introduction

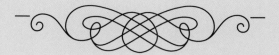

There are hundreds of thousands of flowering plant species in the world. This book uncovers the myths, folklore, cultural associations, and uses of familiar flowers – blooms anyone may find in gardens, along country lanes, or in florists.

Many of these associations are ancient, in some cases dating from Greek, Roman, ancient Chinese, or Native American mythology; others were acquired during the Middle Ages, a rich period for European folklore. As plants were carried from one country to another, perhaps as seeds in a bag of grain or in the luggage of botanical explorers, they took on new associations and uses.

In the 19th century, floriography – the Victorian practice of giving flowers symbolic meanings, creating a "language of flowers", so that the choice of flower conveyed a particular message to the recipient – became popular in Europe and the US. Some of these meanings remain, though others became confused and lost over time.

One of the most striking aspects of the stories in this book is how often plants that are now known to be poisonous were once used in traditional remedies in the countries of their origin – perhaps because people knew how to de-toxify them, so that they could be used safely. It should be stressed, however, that this book is not a herbal guide for medication; the ancient medicinal uses are given only to illustrate the many hidden sides to plants that grow all around the world.

Spring

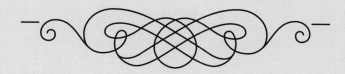

Snowdrop

First flower

According to an ancient Slavic legend, Old Winter loved to linger on Earth, and one year decided with her friends Chill and Wind to remain on Earth forever. That winter was the worst that people had ever experienced, and they even began to run out of food. But then Snowdrop, fed up with waiting underground, poked up his head. The sun warmed the flower and the ice and snow melted.

Native across much of Europe, from the Pyrenees to Ukraine, and naturalized in other places, including Britain and the eastern US and Canada, the snowdrop is the first flower to appear after winter. In a Romanian legend about the snowdrop, every year Sun came to warm the earth in the form of a fairy. One year, the fairy arrived too early and Winter trapped her in the frozen earth. A young hero then fought Winter to set Sun free. Although he was fatally wounded in the battle, his blood melted the ground and snowdrops appeared. It is said that this is a sign that there is always hope, in spite of cold and death. Another Romanian tale maintains that early March is ruled by witches with the power to influence the weather. Romanian men traditionally gave women snowdrops on 1 March in the hope of winning the witches' approval and ensuring a fine spring.

In medieval times, snowdrops were associated with the Virgin Mary, as they were often in flower on Candlemas Day (2 February), marking the ritual purification of Mary 40 days after the birth of Christ. The flowers thus became a symbol of purity. In the Victorian language of flowers, the snowdrop meant hope and purity, but also represented consolation, and it was often planted around graves as a funeral flower.

Spring Crocus

Tribute to a sun goddess

In spring, the yellow blooms of spring crocuses carpet the high plateau of Anatolia, eastern Turkey. The flower (*Crocus ancyrensis*), known as the Ankara crocus, has been celebrated here since the time of the Hittites (1650–1200 BCE). A powerful people mentioned in the Bible and rivals of the ancient Egyptians, the Hittites gathered crocuses to celebrate the sun goddess Arinna during a 38-day festival.

The Anatolian spring has three phases, each said to be marked by a falling ember from the sun. The first, in mid-February, warms the air; the second, a week later, melts frozen water; and the last phase, in early March, warms the cold earth. Even today, during the second phase, children go out from their villages to gather crocus corms and flowers and return to announce spring's arrival with songs. The women then prepare a bulgur pilaf decorated with crocus blooms for the village to share.

The ancient Egyptians, Greeks, Minoans, and Romans also harvested crocuses, especially the saffron crocus (see pages 138–39), which was used in medicines and in cooking. Crocus corms were introduced to the Netherlands from Turkey in the 16th century, and sent to Flemish botanist Carolus Clusius, in Leiden. By 1620, the Dutch Crocus (*C. vernus*) had been developed, helping to launch Holland's bulb industry and introducing the crocus to the rest of the world.

In the Victorian language of flowers, the spring crocus represents "cheerful and youthful gladness", reflecting the exhilarating effect of seeing the colourful crocus pushing up through the winter snow.

Acacia

— ◇ —

Nature's golden cape

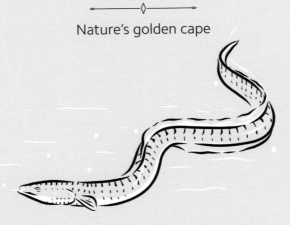

In the wild, mimosa (*Acacia dealbata*), one of 900 species of acacia, grows on the banks of the River Yarra, near Melbourne. To the Aboriginal people of the Wurundjeri clan, who call it Muyan, the appearance of its flowers indicates that it is time to catch eels. When the blossom falls into the water, eels come to feed on the grubs that live in the blooms. Traditionally, the flowers, gum, seed, and wood were used by the Wurundjeri to keep them strong and healthy, just as their Elders' wisdom once did, so this is also a time to remember the Elders.

To early English settlers in Australia the acacias were known as "wattles", as the branches were woven together and sealed with clay to make wattle-and-daub huts. Wattle Day, on 1 September, is a national day to celebrate both being Australian and the start of spring. The Golden Wattle (*A. pycnantha*) is the country's national flower because it is in bloom in most states on 1 September.

Mimosa was introduced into Europe in 1820 and grown for cut flowers in milder parts of Italy and in southern France. In Italy in the 1940s, men in Rome gave the flowers to their female relatives on the

> " As if angels had flown right down out of the softest gold regions of heaven to settle here, in the Australian bush. "

D.H. Lawrence, *Kangaroo*, 1923

Festa della Donna (Women's Day), held on 8 March. Nowadays, women give other women branches of mimosa as a sign of solidarity and friendship.

The African acacia is a thorny tree from Arabia, the source of gum Arabic (a thickening agent) and revered in Judaism as the wood that the Book of Exodus says was used in the Ark of the Covenant. Unrelated to Australian acacia, it has its own genus – *Vachellia*.

Botanical illustration of *Acacia dealbata* (mimosa)

Primrose

First flower of the glade

Sometimes called the English primrose, though it is native to western and southern Europe, *Primula vulgaris* is steeped in British folklore. It was traditionally considered protective, especially against malevolent spirits, and was used in country remedies: an infusion made from primrose petals was drunk as a mild sedative. The flower was also connected with superstitions: the number of primroses gathered in the first spring posy, for example, decided how many chicks a hen would hatch – provided there were no more than 13.

By the 1500s, the primrose had become a popular garden plant, easily transplanted from the hedgerow. Shakespeare often referred to primroses in his plays when he wanted to set a rural scene, confident that his audience would be familiar with them. But primroses also had

❝ When I see the pale yellow blooms and smell their sweetest scent ... I am seven years old again and wandering in that fragrant wood. ❞

Gertrude Jekyll

The Primrose Gatherers, by 19th-century British artist William Stephen Coleman

sinister connotations. According to one legend, young women who died from a form of anaemia known as "green sickness" because it gave them a yellow-green complexion, were changed into primroses.

In the mid-18th century, interest turned to the novelty of hybrids such as the polyanthus, which comes in bright colours and has double flowers, but there was still a great affection for the common primrose. Victorian artists captured this in paintings, such as *The Primrose Gatherers* by William Stephen Coleman and *A Primrose from England* (1855) by Edward Hopley, inspired by a primrose shipped to Australia from England, which conveys the excitement and nostalgia that emigrants felt on seeing a country flower from their homeland.

Primula simply means "first", and there are hundreds of different species of this plant. In the US, *P. meadia*, and *P. hendersonii* on the west coast, are much loved woodland primulas. Their flowers are pink-purple and cyclamen-like, but they have the gentle sedative property of the primrose; the Kashaya Pomo tribe of Sonoma County, California used to hang the flowers of *P. hendersonii* on baby baskets to make the baby sleepy.

Daffodil

◇

Easter's trumpet

As well as giving the daffodil its Latin name of *Narcissus*, the Greek myth of the young man who fell in love with his own reflection (see page 157) influenced the flower's meaning in the Victorian language of flowers. Narcissus in general was associated with "egotism", while the daffodil (*N. pseudonarcissus*) was viewed as a symbol of "regard". The jonquil (*N. jonquilla*), sometimes called the rush daffodil and loved for its scented cup-like flowers, four on each stem, conveyed the more forthright "I desire a return of affection".

The daffodil has long been associated with Easter, and is a symbol of rebirth. In Shakespeare's London, flower girls sold bunches of daffodils as "Lent lilies", because they bloomed during the 40-day period between Ash Wednesday and Easter, a time of fasting and reflection. Originating in southern Portugal and Spain, where it grew on riverbanks and in damp meadows, the wild jonquil

> **❝ Daffodils, that come before the swallow dares, and take the winds of March with beauty. ❞**
>
> **William Shakespeare,** *The Winter's Tale*, 1611

thrived in the wet and windy west of Britain, from Cornwall, up through Wales and north to the Lake District. The daffodil inspired William Wordsworth's poem "I Wandered Lonely as a Cloud", in which the poet describes coming across "a host of golden daffodils" by a Cumbrian lake.

The daffodil is the national flower of Wales, where it begins blooming around 1 March – St David's Day (*Dydd Gwyl Dewi*), when many Welsh people wear a daffodil in their lapel. It is said that the daffodil was not adopted as a national symbol until Victorian times, when it largely replaced the more prosaic leek, traditionally associated with Welsh success in battle.

Violet

◆━━━━━━◆

Love's heady scent

The Nosegay of Violets, by William Worcester Churchill

❝ Forgiveness is the fragrance
the violet sheds on the
heel that has crushed it. ❞

Mark Twain (attributed)

Small and half hidden by heart-shaped leaves, the sweet violet (*V. odorata*) is a symbol of humility and the inspiration for the phrase "shrinking violet" to describe a timorous person. Yet the flower's powerful scent has given it a significance beyond its modest appearance. In ancient Greece, it was the symbol of Athens, associated with Aphrodite, the Greek goddess of love, and used to make love potions and perfumes – as well as a soothing cough syrup.

In medieval Europe, the Viennese court of Leopold VI would ride out to "greet" the first violet of spring before a modest maiden could pick it. And when Joséphine de Beauharnais threw a bunch of sweet violets at the feet of a young Napoleon, he developed a lifelong love of the flower. It is said that he was wearing a locket containing withered violets from Joséphine's grave when he died.

By the late 19th century, Parma violets (*Viola alba*), first bred in Italy, had overtaken the wild flower in both Europe and the US. Larger and showier, and available all year round from nursery greenhouses, they made an attractive corsage, or were sometimes worn on a belt. But by the 1920s, interest even in the Parma violet was on the wane. As the Jazz age beckoned, the heady excitement of a gardenia or orchid pushed the "shrinking violet" back into the shade.

Auricula

◇

Pots of pride and joy

A late 19th-century botanical
print of *Primula auricula*

In the 1570s, waves of Huguenot weavers fled religious persecution
in Europe and sought refuge in Britain. Along with their looms, they
brought little pots of auriculas (*Primula auricula*). Many of the
refugees settled in the East End of London, where an enduring love of
auriculas – a natural hybrid from the mountains of Europe – took root.

In northern England, in 1757, a form of auricula appeared with
green flowers and a ring of "paste" in its centre – a powder that
protects the plant from the sun. Auriculas in other colours, including
slate-blue, brown, and green-grey, drew the interest of collectors.

Traditionally, the plants are displayed in an auricula "theatre" –
wooden shelves with a dark background to show off the jewel-like
flowers. Appealing to everyone, they featured in the backyards of
working-class terraces and in the gardens of fine mansions.

In the Victorian language of flowers, the meaning given to
auriculas is "deserved merit", while red auriculas represent the vice of
"avarice" – perhaps an allusion to the competitive instincts of growers.

Ranunculus

Radiant with charms

The ranunculus ranges from the humble yellow buttercup to the *R. asiaticus*, known as the Persian buttercup, a much larger bloom that comes in many colours, including a spectacular blood-red. According to a Persian folk tale, the *R. asiaticus* sprang up when a handsome prince tried to woo a beautiful nymph with his singing. When she rejected him, he carried on singing and eventually died of a broken heart. The ranunculus bloomed where he fell.

R. asiaticus is a wild species found in Iran, Libya (which has a similar folktale, though it features a Libyan prince), and elsewhere in North Africa and the eastern Mediterranean. Selected forms of the flower, such as double blooms in Italy and semi-doubles in France and Italy, were popular in Europe in the 19th century. To the Victorians, a gift of these flowers meant the recipient was "rich in attractions" or "radiant with charms".

But even the commonplace yellow meadow buttercup (*R. acris*) has a special attribute. According to European folklore, if you hold a buttercup under a child's chin, the golden glow cast by the flower – a reflective property that is unusual in the plant kingdom – is said to indicate a liking for butter.

Plum Blossom

Tree of blessings

Native to central and southern China, the plum tree has been revered for its delicate and fragrant blossom for 3,000 years. For the Chinese, each of the five petals on a single flower represents a blessing: a long life, wealth, health, love of virtue, and a natural death. In Chinese calligraphy, the character for plum blossom expresses the virtues of courage and strength; in Chinese art, the plum tree is one of the "four gentlemen", motifs symbolizing noble virtues, along with the orchid, chrysanthemum, and bamboo.

Chinese art often depicts plum blossom by moonlight. The 17th-century garden designer Ji Cheng described the tree as the "beautiful woman of the forest and moon", and ancient gardens had classical pavilions for viewing plum blossom at night. It is also associated with Princess Shouyang, the flower goddess of the First Moon. According to a story, a single plum blossom dropped onto the forehead of the princess when she fell asleep in the imperial gardens, leaving a pattern of five pink petals on her skin. When her court companions saw this, they painted petals on their own foreheads, setting a trend for *mei hua chuang* – winter plum makeup.

Today, annual plum blossom festivals are enjoyed as social occasions in many parts of China. In homes, it is traditional to arrange a single branch of blossom in a special plum vase known as a *meiping*.

" Its hidden fragrance floats beneath the yellow moon. "

Lin Bu, 10th century

An illustration from *Shi Wu Ben Cao* (*c*. 1500), a book of medicinal plants, shows the collection of "plum rainwater".

Cherry Blossom

◇

First among flowers

When Japan's Emperor Saga held a private viewing of the imperial family's cherry tree blossom (called *sakura* in Japanese) in 812 CE, he started the country's long tradition of *hanami* (flower viewing). At these annual gatherings, courtiers would sit under the cherry blossom and recite or listen to poetry. In "The Tale of Genji" by the 11th-century poet Murasaki Shikibu the trees were portrayed as symbols of youth, romance, and love.

The wider role of *sakura* in Japanese life developed after the Sakoku Edict, which forbade foreign influence, was introduced in 1635, cutting off Japan from the world for more than 200 years. During this time, cultivars from elite gardens in Tokyo known as *sakura-en*, which bore blossom from pure white to dark pink, were planted widely in public places to bring *hanami* to the masses.

Sakura became much more than a sign of spring; the clouds of blossom, which lasted only briefly before they fell, resonated with Japanese beliefs about living beauty being ephemeral. The trees also came to represent what set the Japanese apart. According to a Japanese proverb, "The cherry is the first among

Cherry Blossom Time at Nakanocho in the Yoshiwara (c. 1840–42), by Utagawa Hiroshige

flowers, as the Samurai is the first among men". The life of a Samurai warrior was glorious but often brief, as was that of the cherry blossom.

Author and diplomat Nitobe Inazō described *sakura* as "the favourite of our people and the emblem of our character" in his international bestseller *Bushido: The Soul of Japan* (1900), which shed light on Japanese culture. In 1912, thousands of cherry trees, donated by Japan, were planted around the Tidal Basin in Washington, D.C. Since then, the US has held its own annual cherry blossom festival.

> ❝ Between our two lives
> there is also the life of
> the cherry blossom. ❞

Matsuo Bashō (1644–94)

A carnation in a 16th-century illustrated manuscript

Carnation

Beauty from the Balkans

The wild species of carnation originated in the dry sunny pastures of the Balkans, where the ancient Greek philosopher Theophrastus named it *diosanthos*, meaning "flower of the gods". Some 400 years later, the Roman scholar Pliny the Elder noted its presence in Spain in his *Natural History*. The flower arrived in England from France, its seeds transported on the stones that the Norman invaders brought to build their castles. In the 19th century, a carnation expert found descendants of these plants still thriving on the exposed walls of Dover and Rochester castles in southern England, as well as Fountains Abbey in Yorkshire.

The flower, by now called *dianthus*, was prized in European kitchens, where the clove-scented petals were used to flavour syrups and vinegars. In England in the 16th century, betrothed couples were sometimes served "sops-in-wine" – dianthus petals floating in wine – as a celebratory drink. Other species such as stocks, which shared the desirable clove scent, arrived from Europe and they were collectively known as gillyflowers.

> " The fairest flowers o'th' season
> Are our carnations
> and streaked gillyvors ... "

William Shakespeare, *The Winter's Tale*, 1611

During Tudor times, the English made a distinction between single-flowered "pinks" for planting out in knot gardens or small pots, and the semi-double or double cultivated forms of *D. caryophyllus*, loved for garlands and coronets. The latter became known as coronations and eventually as carnations, though an alternative explanation is that the name carnation is derived from "incarnacyon", meaning "flesh-colour".

In France, the carnation was a favourite at the Court of the Sun King Louis XIV (1638–1715), and a red carnation became a symbol of monarchists. Also in France, a chance seedling from a now-rare tree carnation appeared. The flower smelt of cloves but was large like a rose, so it was named Souvenir de la Malmaison after the rose grown in Empress Joséphine's garden at Château de Malmaison.

> " And in my flower-beds, I think,
> Smile the carnation and the pink. "
>
> **Rupert Brooke**, "The Old Vicarage, Grantchester", 1912

Mother's Day

In the US, carnations are associated with Mother's Day. Anna Marie Jarvis, who introduced the celebration to the country, chose carnations not only for their connection with love but also because they hold on to their petals, just as a mother holds her children. The association is also an allusion to the carnations that were said to spring from the Virgin Mary's tears when Jesus Christ was crucified. Pink carnations represent a mother's love, and white varieties innocence.

In the Victorian language of flowers, carnations represented different kinds of love, according to their colour. A red carnation expressed admiration, but a deep red was an intense love, or signified yearning. A striped carnation expressed regret, or a refusal, while a yellow flower conveyed disappointment or disdain.

In the early 20th century, green carnations, produced by putting the cut stems of white carnations in dyed water, became a symbol of same-sex love when playwright Oscar Wilde, facing prison for charges of "gross indecency", urged his supporters to wear them in their buttonholes. Another famous buttonhole carnation was the "Lamborn Red" presented to US President William McKinley by the plant's breeder, Dr Levi Lamborn, prior to a debate. McKinley continued to wear a red buttonhole, calling it his good-luck charm, a superstition that may have had some merit. On 14 September 1901, McKinley was assassinated moments after removing the flower from his lapel to give to a young admirer.

Carnations have been symbols of political rebellion too. In the Netherlands, the white carnation is worn in memory of the Resistance in World War II. In Portugal, red carnations represent the 1974 military and civil coup, often referred to as the Carnation Revolution, because carnations were worn by the soldiers and placed in the muzzles of their guns. Red carnations symbolize socialism and the labour movement, and are sometimes worn on 1 May – International Workers' Day.

Magnolia

❧

The "tree lily"

" The magnolia blooms
toss like white horses. "

Frank Kingdom-Ward, 1930

W hen the first *Magnolia x soulangeana* flowered near Paris in 1826, it caused a sensation with its huge and copious blooms. Created by botanist Étienne Soulange-Bodin, a former cavalry officer in Napoleon's army, it was a hybrid of two Chinese species – *M. liliiflora* and *M. denudata*.

In China and Japan, magnolias have long been associated with purity and nobility. A magnolia in flower was considered a suitable gift for an emperor, sometimes from the governor of an important province. Wild magnolias cling to the sides of the Himalayan foothills and have been grown as cultivated trees in Buddhist temples and gardens since ancient times. The flowers and flower buds of the dark-pink *M. liliiflora* are used in traditional medicine, to remedy the stagnation of *qi* – the vital energy that is said to circulate through the body – and to treat sinus troubles.

Magnolias are also native to the Americas. Here they mostly flower in summer, but the rare *M. macrophylla var. dealbata* is an exception and blooms from April. Spanish scientific explorer Francisco Hernández spotted this Mexican species on an expedition in 1570 and noted that the Aztecs called the beautiful tree Eloxochitl, after which many girl babies were named. This species of the cloud forest is endangered, but Oaxaca locals care for the trees and use its creamy white flowers to decorate churches and crosses at Easter time.

Tulip

Blazing beauty

" The flames in our fireplaces
are the tulip gardens of winter. "

Ancient Persian poem

For nearly 1,000 years, tulips have symbolized love and devotion. A red tulip with a dark centre was said to represent burning love and the ashes of a burnt heart. For the Victorians, yellow tulips signified hopeless love.

There are many romantic tales about tulips, especially in the home of wild tulips – the remote mountain ranges of Central Asia, where China, Russia, and Afghanistan meet. In the 11th century, the Seljuks took wild tulips with them when they moved out of the region to conquer most of Anatolia and northern Persia.

According to Persian folklore, the first tulips arose from the spilt blood of a doomed lover – but whose blood? It depends on who is telling the story. A 12th-century poem, itself a re-telling of an even older epic, starts as a love story between King Khosrow and his wife, Princess Shirin, and becomes a love triangle involving a stonemason, Farhad. In one version, flowers spring from Farhad's blood when he throws himself off a cliff. In others, Shirin's blood mingles with his when she sees his body and follows suit. In yet another version, Shirin ends her life when Khosrow is killed. No matter which tale is told, the ending is always the same – the blood of the lover turns into a bright red tulip.

In the Caucasus, a magical Georgian legend explains the origin of a tulip species with pink splashed leaves. According to the story, cruel King Morphiliziy kills a man in a duel and then tries to marry the man's daughter. But Nina's heart belongs to another, and her old nurse helps the girl escape with her true love. When Morphiliziy finds them sheltering in the home of a kindly man, he cuts off the man's head and a black cloud covers the corpse. When this clears, a white tulip stands in place of the body. The king then turns on the nurse, beheading her as well, and her blood splashes the centre of the tulip, turning it red and marking the leaves with pink stripes. Next, the king attacks the lovers, who turn into butterflies and hide in the leaves, leading the enraged king to become a blazing fire that is only extinguished when the nurse's body turns into torrential rain. Free at last, the couple take the tulip to a new land where it grows into a whole field of tulips.

The tulip was also held in high regard in the Ottoman Empire, where it was the symbol of the ruling Osman family. From the 16th century, the tulip motif was embroidered on fabrics, woven into carpets, and painted on tiles, including those at the Topkapı Palace. By the 1630s, the Turkish capital, Constantinople, had flower shops selling tulips.

The reign of Ottoman Sultan Ahmed III (1703–30) was peaceful and prosperous, until he was undone by his passion for tulips, a craze that was reflected in an abundance of tulip gardens. After ordering millions of tulip bulbs from Holland at

Tulipmania

In 17th-century Holland, wealthy burghers became obsessed with "broken" tulips, which have striped petals. The very rich commissioned artists, including Ambrosius Bosschaert and Jan Brueghel to paint them. Trading in the bulbs led to tulipmania, when sky-high prices (one bulb exceeded the annual salary of a skilled worker) led to a stock market bubble. Because the "breaking" is caused by a virus, these bulbs are no longer sold, but virus-free varieties, such as Flaming Parrot, have been bred to look like them.

Tiles decorated with tulips in the Rustem Pasha Mosque, Istanbul

vast expense, he had to raise taxes to pay for them, which led his people to rise up and depose him, ending what became known as the Tulip Era in Turkey.

In Europe, the tulip was considered exotic. "Broken" tulips, whose petals have a striped pattern, were a particular fascination (see left). Centuries later, the Victorians borrowed the Persian association of red tulips as a "declaration of love".

Today, tulips are given during Nowruz, the Persian New Year, which falls on the Spring Equinox. An Iranian song for Nowruz still lauds the tulip: "This spring be your good luck, the tulip fields be your joy".

> ❝ The tulip in her lifted chalice bears
> A dewy wine of Heaven's minist'ring ... ❞
>
> **Hafez Shirazi,** Persian poet, 14th century

Pussy Willow

◦———◇———◦

Cats' paws and rabbits' tails

Several folktales attempt to explain how pussy willow (*Salix caprea* in Europe and *S. discolor* in North America) got its common name, all inspired by the silky-grey buds that grow on the male plants and bloom into fluffy catkins. In Rhode Island, in the US, the Narragansett people tell a story about a rabbit that climbed onto the willow when it snowed, then slid off when it thawed, leaving tufts of fur behind.

On the same theme in Polish folklore, some kittens were chasing butterflies along a riverbank when they fell into the fast-flowing current. Hearing the mother cat crying helplessly, the willows growing alongside the river lowered their branches into the water. The kittens gripped them tightly and clambered to safety on shore. Ever since then, it is said, the willow tree has sprouted a layer of silky fur in spring.

Spring comes late to Poland and other eastern European countries, and Christians here gather branches of pussy willow to celebrate Palm Sunday at the start of Holy Week. Then on Dyngus Day (Easter Monday), young people playfully flick each other with willow switches and throw water over one another to assert their hopes of romance.

Pussy willow also features in several other northern European countries at Easter. On Easter Day in Ukraine, for example, churchgoers tap each other with the blessed branches of the tree and say, "Be as big as the willow, healthy as water, rich as the earth". In Finland, children traditionally dress up as Easter witches and go door to door wishing people good luck and trading decorated branches of pussy willow for coins and treats.

Anemone

Flower of the winds

The ancient Greeks called these flowers *anemos* after the Anemoi – the gods of the four winds. According to Greek mythology, red anemones formed when Aphrodite, the goddess of love, shed tears on her mortal lover Adonis's grave, accounting for one of the plant's other names – Adonis flowers. In the Victorian language of flowers, anemones symbolized forsaken love or the death of a loved one.

There are some 120 species of anemone. *Anemone coronaria*, also called the poppy anemone for its jewel-like colours and black button centres, are native to the central and eastern Mediterranean. In the 12th century, Christian crusaders attempting to expel Muslim forces from Jerusalem called these blooms "blood drops of Christ". It is said that when the Bishop of Pisa returned to Italy after fighting in the Holy Land, he filled his ship with soil as ballast. When this was unloaded at Pisa, the seeds it contained were dispersed, thus introducing anemones to Italy.

Anemones were first cultivated as garden flowers in Italy in the late 16th century. In the following centuries, plant breeders in various countries created new varieties, including today's florist favourites: the single-flowered French de Caen group, which were introduced in the 18th century, and the Irish St Brigid group of double or semi-double flowers, which appeared in the 1880s.

Camellia

A chic rosette

The Japanese name for *Camellia japonica* is *tsubaki* meaning "tree with shining leaves". Valued for its seed oil, it was said to be the geisha's secret to fine skin. The flowers symbolize love, happiness, and a long life, so they are often given as wedding gifts and used in *ikebana* – artistic arrangements of blossoms, branches, and leaves. An exception is the white-flowered camellia, which is associated with death.

A feature of japonicas is that the flowers drop suddenly rather than petal by petal, a peculiarity celebrated in many haikus (short poems). It is said that during the Edo Period (1603–1867), the falling red flowers reminded the samurai of their duty to behead wrongdoers. Because of this, they preferred Higo camellias (from the Higo province of Japan), which are symbols of bravery.

> **"** White camellias
> Only the sound of their falling
> Moonlit night. **"**

Ranko Takakuwa (1726–98)

Ornamental camellias arrived in Europe in 1692, and North America in the late 1700s. Wrongly thought to be tender, they were initially grown inside the glasshouses of the wealthy. Most people saw the flower depicted on wallpaper or ceramics before seeing the real plant.

Camellia blooms were popular as corsages and buttonholes in the 19th century; their meanings – "lovely" or "adorable" – were positive but general. However, in Brazil, before the abolition of slavery in 1888, the white camellia was a symbol for abolitionists. Portuguese

Choosing **(1864)**, by British artist George Frederic Watts

businessman José de Seixas Magalhães gave refuge to enslaved people on a settlement known as Quilombo do Leblon, where they grew white camellias commercially. Supporters wore a white camellia and planted them in their front gardens.

One day in 1913, Coco Chanel pinned a neat *C. japonica 'Alba Plena'* to her belt. She loved the shape of the white flower as well as the fact that it had no scent; she went on to make it a symbol of the Chanel brand.

Forget-me-not

❖ ❖ ❖

Keeping faith

A popular folktale in many European countries tells how a medieval knight in armour was walking with his lady by a fast-flowing river when she spotted a cluster of pretty blue flowers growing by the water's edge. To please her, the knight reached out to grab them, but weighed down by his armour, was pulled under the water and carried away by the current. His last words to his love were "Forget me not".

The pretty forget-me-not (*Myosotis scorpioides*) became a symbol of public as well as personal fidelity. When Henry Bolingbroke, was banished from England by King Richard II in

A German postcard dating from the 1930s

40

1398, his forget-me-not emblem represented mutual loyalty for his followers. When he returned to England to overthrow Richard and become King Henry IV, he promoted the humble flower to a royal symbol.

The Victorians loved the melodrama of the legends associated with such a dainty little flower and endowed it not only with the meanings "true love" and "remember me" but also with the virtues of loyalty and faithfulness. Forget-me-nots were often depicted on cards and decorative objects, such as fine porcelain, enamel boxes, and jewellery.

Although forget-me-nots are much-loved wildflowers in Europe, they are sometimes considered invasive weeds elsewhere, as are true forget-me-not (*M. arvensis*) and woodland species (*M. sylvatica*) in the US. In Alaska, the alpine forget-me-not (*M. alpestris*) is a wildflower of the mountain meadows. It was first adopted as an emblem of the early pioneers and later became the official state flower. Women would wear the flowers as a sign of devotion and faithfulness when their husbands were away from home.

Similar to forget-me-nots, but with four petals rather than five, are bluets (*Houstonia*), a much-loved wildflower of Canada and the eastern US. Also known as Quaker ladies because the shape of the bloom is similar to hats once worn by women of the Quaker faith, the flowers symbolize contentment. The Cherokee people used an infusion of bluets to cure bedwetting; the flowers were brewed into a tea, which was said to strengthen the bladder.

> " She is dressed in blue, with blue flowers in her hair – forget-me-nots – as if SHE had any need to wear forget-me-nots. "

Charles Dickens, *David Copperfield*, 1849

Mountain Laurel

Poisoned beauty

Kalmia latifolia, known as mountain laurel

E arly European settlers in the eastern US learned the hard way that the mountain laurel (*kalmia latifolia*) was toxic. A number of people in Philadelphia died after eating game birds that had been feeding on its berries; and some even died after consuming honey made from the flower's nectar. Its effects on animals led to its nickname "sheepskill". Yet Native Americans, who had long known that it was poisonous, used the leaves in traditional medicine. The Cherokee people made an infusion to relieve pain; the Abnaki and Algonquin peoples of Quebec took a snuff of crushed leaves for colds.

　　The plant's habit of forming dense thickets led to it being called "laurel hell" among settlers in the Appalachians. In Pennsylvania, where it is the state flower, forestry workers refer to it as an "ankle breaker" because of its twisting roots.

Alpenrose

Queen of the Alps

The Swiss have a great affection for this small, mountain-dwelling rhododendron. Many hotels are named after the flower, and a magazine called *Alpenrose* celebrates traditional Swiss culture. In folklore, it was thought that witches could use the alpenrose, also known as the thunder rose, to conjure up thunderstorms, and that anyone holding the flower during a storm would be struck by lightning. According to one legend, a young girl, who knew about the risk, gave her beloved an alpenrose flower because he had annoyed her. When the young man proudly put it in the band of his hat, he was struck by lightning, as foretold, and the devastated girl died of guilt.

The alpenrose (*Rhododendron ferrugineum*) was a favourite flower of the 19th-century English art critic John Ruskin, who referred to it as the "queen of the Alps". He detested the name rhododendron, so he called the plant "aurora" (meaning dawn). The Victorian meaning for all rhododendrons was "danger beware", as the plants are toxic if swallowed. Nevertheless, the alpenrose was used in traditional medicine in Switzerland and Germany. Honey made from the nectar of alpenrose – sometimes called "mad honey" – is said to be an aphrodisiac.

Pansy

Love's idleness

A member of the *Viola* genus, the pansy has long been thought of as an aphrodisiac. One of its common names is heart's ease, and Shakespeare knew the pansy as love-in-idleness. In *A Midsummer Night's Dream*, Oberon, the King of the Fairies, sends his servant Puck to find a flower whose juice would make "man or woman madly dote upon the next live creature that it sees". After juice from a pansy is sprinkled on the eyelids of the sleeping Queen Titania, she wakes to fall in love with the labourer Bottom – who is disguised as an ass.

The modern pansy evolved through hybridization of the wild species (*Viola tricolor*). Its name comes from the French word *pensées*, meaning idle thoughts, perhaps because the flowers bow their heads as if deep in thought. Up until the mid-19th century, a

" The beauteous pansies rise In purple, gold, and blue, With tints of rainbow hue. "

Thomas J. Ouseley, 1849

SPRING

typical show pansy would have had a flat face and been "as big as a penny piece". Dark markings – in the form of blotches or enhanced veins known as whiskers were popular, and some pansies were described as looking like cats' faces. Later in the century, flowers without markings were preferred.

Pansies were popular tokens of friendship in Victorian times, given to someone as a simple way to show that they were in your thoughts. They were considered cottage-garden plants associated with domestic bliss; blue pansies meant faithfulness and yellow ones represented happiness.

Pansies also have a long history as a medicinal plant in Europe and beyond. All parts growing above ground are safe to eat. A syrup made from the flowers was a handy remedy to ease sore throats and chest complaints such as asthma.

Stock

◆————◆————◆

Scented beauty

Known for their heady fragrance, stocks are also sometimes called gillyflowers, a term that once referred to any flower with a clove-like scent. Native to south and western Europe and the Arabian peninsula, stock-gillyflowers were introduced to England in the 13th century. In the 16th century, they were grown on London balconies to conceal the smells rising from the city's streets and sewers.

Some stocks were considered to have stimulating properties; *Matthiola incana* is named after Pierandrea Mattiola, a 16th-century Italian botanist and doctor, who prescribed its seeds as an aphrodisiac. The French developed "ten-week stocks", which flower within ten weeks of being sown, a process that had previously taken two years. This explains why ten-week stocks signified promptness in the Victorian language of flowers. The meaning ascribed to *M. incana* was "lasting beauty".

Night-scented stock (*M. longipetela*) releases its sweet perfume at night in order to attract nocturnal pollinators such as moths. Its relative, sweet rocket (*Hesperis matronalis*) gives off a similar scent and was known as dame's rocket or dame's violet in the 19th century, because women liked to keep vases of the flowers in their homes. It was said to represent deceit in the Victorian language of flowers, because, like *M. longipetela*, it gives off no scent at all during the daytime but is beautifully fragrant after dark.

Common Daisy

◆

Love's oracle

Referred to as the "eie of daie" (eye of day) by English medieval author Geoffrey Chaucer for its habit of opening at dawn and closing at dusk, the common daisy (*Bellis perennis*) represented purity in ancient times. In Roman mythology, the nymph Belides turned herself into a daisy to protect her virtue from Vertumnus, god of the seasons. The Celts believed that daisies were the spirits of babies who had died, so the flower became a symbol of childhood innocence. In Norse mythology, the daisy was a sacred flower of Freya, goddess of fertility, mothers, and childbirth.

English herbalist Nicholas Culpeper's *The Complete Herbal* (1653) said of the daisy "nature has made [it] common because it may be useful". Remedies included applying the daisy's crushed leaves to wounds to heal them and using an infusion of the plant as an eyewash.

The much-loved custom of pulling off the petals of a daisy in turn while saying "Loves me" and "Loves me not" until only one petal remains, which determines whether a person returns your affection, is said to have arisen in either France or Germany. In the Victorian language of flowers, the receipt of daisies declared "I share your sentiments" – so there was no need to pull off the petals to find out.

Peony

Esteemed flower of China

One of the earliest references to the peony is in the *Shi Jing* (*Book of Odes*), an anthology of Chinese poetry dating from the 8th to 7th centuries BCE. The Chinese peony (*Paeonia lactiflora*) was a metaphor for a blushing girl and reflected the tradition of young men and women exchanging peonies as a sign of love. The peony (*shao yao*) was said to be a "binding herb" that bound the two.

In later centuries, peonies were at the top of the Chinese hierarchy of flowers and often shown alongside a peacock or phoenix in paintings, because these were considered aristocratic. The Hui people of western China sing songs about a peacock that falls in love with a peony or that compare a lover to a peacock or a flowering peony.

> " For whom do they shed
> their petals and leaves
> For whom do they bloom? "
>
> **Emperor Yang** (569–618 CE)

The peeled and dried roots of peonies have been used in traditional Chinese medicine for 1,200 years, particularly to treat rheumatoid arthritis, fever, and spasms. The roots are also found in the "four things soup", the ingredients of a tonic used to cure gynaecological problems. Recent research has found the dried root contains phytoestrogens, which have a similar structure to human oestrogen.

Cultivated forms of the peony arrived in the West in the 19th century. According to some sources, the European peony (*P. officinalis*) is named after the mythical Greek figure Paeon, physician to the gods. Another story describes how a nymph called Paeonia attracted the attention of Apollo. When she realized that Aphrodite was watching them, the nymph's pleasure in their flirting turned to embarrassment, giving rise to the Victorian meaning for the flower – bashfulness.

Summer

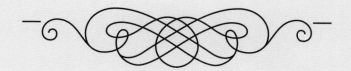

Poppy

❧

The sleepy siren

The red field poppy (*Papaver rhoeas*) and the opium poppy (*P. somniferum*) are flowers of Mediterranean origin that have spread to the rest of the world. Their success is partly due to the vast number of tiny seeds that they disperse from their spherical seed pods.

The ancient Greeks believed that crops would not grow without the presence of red poppies and associated the flower with Demeter, goddess of fertility. They also believed that poppies grew in the land of the dead, having observed them on battlefields, and so linked them to Demeter's daughter Persephone – queen of the underworld.

The poppy first arrived in China as a weed seed in grain crops, and became popular for its bright red flowers. It was named *yumeiren*, meaning Yu the Beauty, to honour Consort Yu, who fought in battle

Poppies in ink on silk, by Sakai Doitsu, 19th century

" Through the dancing poppies stole
A breeze, most softly lulling to my soul. "

John Keats, *Endymion*, 1818

> " In Flanders fields the poppies blow
> Between the crosses, row on row ... "

John McCrae, 1915

alongside her lover, warlord Xiang Yu, in the third-century BCE. The poppy was said to have sprung from her blood after she died by suicide so that Xiang Yu would not be distracted from his mission.

Field poppies provided pain relief for everyday ailments, such as toothache, earache, and sore throats, in many ancient cultures. People also made a sedative or relaxant by steeping fresh or dried petals in water or wine. For a more potent narcotic, the "milk", or sap, of the opium poppy was extracted after petal fall. In 13th-century China, the double-flowered opium poppy was called *dayanhua* (big-tobacco flower), indicating that it was considered a more powerful intoxicant than tobacco. In California, the Kitanemuk people used the roots to create a mild narcotic and made an extract from the seeds to relieve headaches; the Luiseño people chewed its petals like chewing-gum.

In the Victorian flower language, the red poppy was a symbol of consolation, the large scarlet poppy (*P. orientale*) conveyed fantastic extravagance, and the white poppy represented sleep or "my antidote", perhaps in recognition of the opium poppy's sedative qualities. In World War I, the battles in northern France and Belgium brought the buried seeds of the field poppy to the surface and flowers bloomed between the lines of trenches. There were so many red flowers that they seemed to mirror the blood spilled and the many lives lost. In 1921, the poppy became the flower of remembrance for the war dead of the UK and countries of the British Commonwealth.

Himalayan blue poppy
— ⟨∿⟩ —

So rarely seen that it was long thought to be a myth, the Himalayan blue poppy grows in the high mountain passes of the eastern Himalayas and Tibet, China, and is the national flower of Bhutan. Originally thought to be a subspecies of another poppy, it is now classified as a unique species called *Meconopsis gakyidiana* – *gakyid* meaning happiness and *diana* meaning flower in Dzongkha, the official language of Bhutan.

Cornflower

True blue

In the US, the brilliant blue cornflower is known as bachelor's button, reputedly because young men wore the flower in their buttonholes when they were in love. If the bloom lasted, there was hope the man's feelings were returned; if it wilted, his love was unrequited.

A native of western Asia, the cornflower, which often grows wild among cereal crops, gradually spread around the Mediterranean region, its seeds often carried in imported grain. In ancient Egypt, where it was a similar colour to the revered blue lotus, the flower was held in high esteem and became a symbol of life and fertility. When Egyptologist Howard Carter opened Tutankhamun's tomb in 1922, he found cornflowers among the funerary bouquets and wreaths.

The Latin name, *Centaurea*, comes from the flower's association with the centaur Chiron of Greek myth. Chiron was renowned for his wisdom. When he was accidentally wounded by a poisoned arrow shot by Heracles, he used cornflowers to heal his wounds. The flowers are still used medicinally, to relieve tired eyes and heal mouth ulcers.

In medieval Europe, the cornflower was considered a nuisance. Not only did it reduce the yields of valuable crops, but the flowers' tough stems blunted the blades of scythes, earning it the nickname "hurt-sickle". Its reputation was redeemed in 19th-century Germany after Queen Louise of Prussia hid her children in a field of cornflowers while fleeing from Napoleon's army. When her son became Emperor Wilhelm I, he made the cornflower the national emblem in honour of his mother. The cornflower is also the national flower of Estonia and often features in its folk art. Young girls in the country wear cornflowers in traditional garlands at folk festivals.

" And for the blue
that o'er the sea is born,
A brighter rises in
our standing corn. **"**

Anne Finch, c.1685

Ancient Rose

Hedonist of the hedgerow

We know that the ancient Greeks grew roses and foraged for wild briars from the writings of philosopher and father of botany Theophrastus, who wrote about making rose crowns and garlands. He also recommended fragrant roses as an effective way to remove odours from clothes and bedding, and thought that the roses with the sweetest perfumes were grown in Cyrene (modern Libya). His description of a wild briar rose as "one whose roots would cure the bite of a mad dog" provided the name dog rose and the botanical label *Rosa canina*.

In Greek mythology, Aphrodite, the goddess of love and beauty, was associated with roses (as was her Roman counterpart, Venus). In one account, red roses grew from the ground where Aphrodite's tears

The Roman leader Elagabalus showers guests with rose petals in a painting by 19th-century Anglo-Dutch artist Sir Lawrence Alma-Tadema.

mingled with the blood of her wounded mortal lover, Adonis. In a second version, she pricked her foot on a white rose while racing to Adonis's side, and her blood turned the white flower red. Another myth told of her son Eros, who gave a rose to Harpocrates, god of silence, to remind him to keep the indiscretions of Aphrodite and the other gods a secret.

> " If Zeus had willed it so
> That o'er the flowers one
> flower should reign a queen,
> I know, ah well I know
> The rose, the rose, that
> royal flower had been! "

Sappho (attributed), 6th century BCE

Fresco from Pompeii, first century CE

“ With sweet musk roses
and with eglantine:
There sleeps Titania
sometime of the night,
Lull'd in these flowers
with dances and delight. ”

William Shakespeare, *A Midsummer Night's Dream,* 1605

Fairy-tale blooms

The briar rose was immortalized in the popular Grimm's fairy tale *Little Briar Rose*, now better known as *Sleeping Beauty*, in which a princess sleeps under an evil spell for 100 years in a castle hidden by briar roses. The story has inspired many works of art, including ballet music by Tchaikovsky; *The Legend of the Briar Rose* by the pre-Raphaelite artist Edward Burne-Jones; and several films, beginning with Walt Disney's animated *Sleeping Beauty* in 1959.

In the Middle Ages, there was an understanding that conversations held "under a rose" were confidential. This could have been a real rose suspended from the ceiling or, more likely, a painted or carved rose. The Latin *sub rosa* is still in use today as a legal term meaning confidential.

The roses grown by the ancients were probably forms of European wild species such as briars and gallicas. The fruits, known as hips, of the briars – prickly, rampant plants with single flowers – were foraged to make syrups. Evidence that the Romans grew gallica-type roses comes from a Roman tomb found in Hawara, Egypt, in the late 1880s. Inside was a burial wreath of flowers including rosebuds, shrunken but well preserved, dating from the second century CE.

Rose garlands were also made for Roman festivals, where they were worn by revellers and offered to the deities. The riotous Rosalia festival, held in May, was dedicated to the rose harvest. Rose-growing, particularly for garlands, was a lucrative business and accounts of how to grow and prepare flowers for such festivals survive.

Bacchus, the god of wine, was often depicted wearing a rose garland at such festivals, and roses gradually became associated with excess. In the first century CE, Emperor Nero took to showering his guests with rose petals, as Elagabalus reputedly did a century later. Cleopatra famously scattered rose petals liberally across the floors of her palace so that Mark Antony would think of her every time he smelled the scent of roses.

Jasmine

Star of heaven

The name jasmine, from the old Persian word *yāsamin*, means gift from God, reflecting this star-like flower's association with the divine qualities of purity and beauty. Native to central and Southeast Asia (*Jasminum officinale*) and the Indian subcontinent (*J. sambac*), it symbolizes purity in the Hindu and Buddhist faiths, and jasmine is laid in temples as offerings. It is also one of the flowers that decorate the bow and arrows of Kamadeva, the Hindu god of human love.

In the 17th century, Peter II of Portugal gave a jasmine plant from Goa, a Portuguese colony in India, to Cosimo III de' Medici, Grand Duke of Tuscany. When Cosimo's gardener stole a spray of the precious plant for his fiancée, she propagated and sold it, making enough money for the lovers to marry. Meanwhile, Cosimo's physician, Francesco Redi, created a jasmine-flavoured chocolate drink made by layering jasmine flowers with cocoa chips, a concoction that took 12 days to prepare.

Jasmine is also a key component of the world's top perfumes, including one of its most famous – Chanel No. 5. Some 8,000 jasmine blooms are needed to extract 1 ml (0.03 fl oz) of "absolute" – the most concentrated essence of a flower, which is used in perfumes.

An Indian miniature, c. 1800, depicts a woman under jasmine blooms.

"" Yet my memory is still sweet with the first white jasmines that I held in my hand when I was a child. ""

Rabindranath Tagore, 1861

Gallica Rose

The apothecary rose

The Gallica rose (*Rosa gallica*) is the oldest cultivated form of the rose. It is also known as the apothecary rose, because its semi-double flowers provided medieval herbalists with extra petals to make their rose-based remedies, which ranged from rosewater and oils to seed powders. The town of Provins, near Paris, grew the Gallica rose commercially from the late 13th century; its main street was dominated by apothecaries selling rose-based treatments.

In the poem *Roman de la Rose* (1225–37), written in Old French, a man seeks to claim a rose growing in a walled garden. In the first half, written by Guillaume de Lorris, the man fails in his quest. In the second half, completed 40 years later by Jean de Meun, the walls

> **"** Women are as roses, whose
> fair flower, being once displayed,
> doth fall that very hour. **"**

William Shakespeare, *Twelfth Night,*1602

are destroyed and the man takes the rosebud. This popular poem
was imitated in Europe for centuries, with innocent terms such as
"plucking a rosebud" or "deflowering a rose" suddenly acquiring sexual
connotations. Critics included poet Christine de Pizan, who challenged
their misogynistic tone. In her poem *Le Dit de la Rose* (1401), roses
are only bestowed on knights who uphold a woman's virtue.

The pink and white striped *R. gallica versicolor* was a natural
mutation of a red gallica rose that emerged in England in 1583. Legend
tells of a similar rose placed on the 12th-century tomb of Rosamond
Clifford, the mistress of King Henry II and purportedly murdered by
the queen. The association is said to account for the flower's other
names – Fair Rosamond's rose and Rosa mundi (rose of the world).

Aquilegia

✦ ✦ ✦

A dove in flight

The cosy image of columbine (Aquilegia) as a cottage garden favourite belies its history as a medicine, love potion, and poison. In North America, the Meskwaki people of the St Lawrence River Valley, Ontario, used the seeds of red columbine (*A. canadensis*) as an aphrodisiac, and the Omaha people of the Ohio River Valley and the Pawnee people of the North Platte River, Nebraska, prepared infusions of seeds as love potions or to alleviate fevers. The Thompson people, now called the Ntlakapamux, of British Columbia, smeared the roots of *A. formosa* between the legs of men and horses to boost their stamina.

In Europe, aquilegia was known to be toxic if ingested, but *A. vulgaris* was also known as *herba leonis* (lion plant), an allusion to a belief that lions ate aquilegia to recover their strength in spring. It was said that a person could gain the courage of a lion by rubbing the plant between their hands.

The shape of the flower – its petals look like a cluster of doves in flight – inspired its common name columbine (from *columba*, Latin for dove), giving rise to an association with the Holy Spirit in Christianity. The shape of the petals also earned it the nickname "jester's hat", and by extension the meaning "folly" in the 19th-century language of flowers. The colour was also thought significant. A red aquilegia meant "anxious and trembling" while purple meant "resolved to win". In 1899, Colorado chose *A. caerulea* as its state flower because its blue and white petals were said to evoke the snow-capped Rocky Mountains and its yellow centre the state's history of gold mining.

Lady's Slipper Orchid

The moccasin flower

Lady's slipper orchid

In North America, the lady's slipper orchid (*Cypripedium calceolus*) is known as the moccasin flower in honour of an Ojibwe legend. According to the story, one winter, an Ojibwe village was hit by a plague and many people died. A woman went to the next village to collect medicine, but on her return she collapsed, her feet swollen from frostbite. When the villagers found the woman, they carried her home and wrapped her feet in deerskins. When she died, the deerskins turned into shoe-shaped flowers.

Native American people such as the Cherokee and the Ojibwe once relied on the roots of the yellow slipper orchid to bring down fevers and ease labour pains. They also used the pink lady's slipper orchid to treat stomach cramps. Native Americans and European settlers used the dried roots of both species as a remedy for anxiety.

Lilac

Wild at heart

In the Balkan Mountains of southeast Europe, local people used to hollow out small lilac branches to make pipes for smoking. The 18th-century Swedish botanist Carl Linnaeus assigned the name Syringa to the plant from the Greek word *syrinx*, meaning pipe. According to Greek myth, Syrinx was a nymph who was pursued by the satyr Pan. When she asked the river nymphs to help her escape, they transformed her into reeds, but Pan took the reeds and cut them into panpipes. Children in Austria and Germany were still making whistles from lilac stems in the early 20th century.

Loved for its strong fragrance, lilac (*S. vulgaris*) was fashionable in Europe from the 1870s until the early 20th century, during which time French plant breeders Victor Lemoine and his son Émile introduced many new cultivars. These new lilacs arrived in North America with the early European immigrants and thrived in Canada and the colder parts of the US. As early as 1753, John Bartram, an American botanist, noted that lilacs were growing profusely there.

In the Victorian language of flowers, the lilac was associated with humility; white-flowered lilac meant youthful innocence, suitable for a flower girl or bridesmaid to carry, while the purple

> " When the light summer wind
> stirred amidst the trees of the garden,
> there came through the open door
> the heavy scent of the lilac. "

Oscar Wilde, *The Picture of Dorian Gray*, 1891

variety signified the "first emotions of love". At the start of *The Picture of Dorian Gray*, Oscar Wilde describes his then innocent protagonist "burying his face in the great cool lilac blossoms, feverishly drinking in their perfume, as if it had been wine."

The heavy scent of lilacs is famously evocative. When President Abraham Lincoln was assassinated in 1865, American poet Walt Whitman was at his mother's house. On hearing the news, he went into her garden and wrote the elegy "When Lilacs Last in the Dooryard Bloom'd". Years later, he said that the sight and smell of lilacs always took him back to that tragic event.

Damask Rose

Perfume of the Middle East

According to Persian legend, a snow-white rose was so beautiful that the nightingale became intensely devoted to her. He sang sweetly of his longing while fluttering so close that her thorns pierced his flesh and splashes of blood turned the petals crimson. This close connection between the rose, symbolizing beauty and perfection, and the nightingale, representing devotional love – known as *gol o bolbol* – has inspired Persian art and literature.

Damask rose is a Western name for what is known in Iran, where it originates, as the *gol-e Mohammadi*, or Mohammed rose. According to Islamic tradition, this deeply fragrant flower sprang from beads of the Prophet's sweat, giving its essence, either as rosewater or oil, a spiritual significance. When rosewater was exported beyond the Middle East, first eastwards to the Indian subcontinent and later to Europe, other cultures used it in different ways. In the Hindu faith, for example, the rose is considered to be Lord Krishna's favourite flower, and Hindu altars are washed with rosewater.

In Judaism, the rose is considered to be a metaphor for God's love for the people of Israel. They are the chosen, "the rose among the thorns". On the Jewish holiday of Shavuot in late May or early June, which celebrates Moses receiving the Torah (God's law), roses are used to decorate homes and synagogues.

> " The rose has flushed red,
> the bud has burst,
> And drunk with joy is
> the nightingale. "

Hafez Shirazi, Persian poet, 14th century

An image from a 17th-century edition of the *Gulistan* (*Rose Garden*) by 13th-century Persian poet Sa'di

White Lily

Pure beauty

Loved for its large, trumpet-shaped flowers and heady fragrance, the white lily (*Lilium candidum*), traditionally symbolizes purity. The lover in the Bible's Song of Solomon says of the beloved, "Like a lily among thorns is my darling among maidens".

One of the oldest known flowers and native to the eastern Mediterranean, the white lily has been cultivated for at least 3,000 years. To the Minoans, the flower symbolized royal majesty as well as purity; paintings of lilies appear in 15th-century BCE frescoes in the throne room of the ancient Minoan palace of Knossos on Crete. In Greek mythology, the lily sprang up when drops of milk fell from the breast of Hera, wife of Zeus and goddess of marriage and childbirth.

By around 1300, the white lily had become associated with the Virgin Mary, and featured in paintings of the Virgin for the next 500 years. Renaissance paintings of the Annunciation – the moment when the angel Gabriel tells Mary she will conceive the son of God – often include a vase of three white lilies to represent her purity. For this reason, *L. candidum* later became known as the Madonna lily, though religious art also shows St Anthony of Padua holding lilies. It is said that in 1680, a cut lily placed in the hand of a statue of St Anthony in Mentosca d'Agesco, Austria stayed fresh for a year, and then grew two more blooms.

Other white lilies include the Easter (*Lilium longiflorum*) and regal lilies, which originated in Japan and China respectively, and were introduced to the West in the

Detail from Filippino Lippi's *Annunciation with St John the Baptist and St Andrew* (1483)

> **"**... the Lily white shall in love delight,
> Nor a thorn nor a threat
> stain her beauty bright. **"**

William Blake, "The Lily", 1794

19th century. The Easter lily, known for its strong sweet scent, became a symbol of the Resurrection and is widely used to decorate churches on Easter Day. The regal or royal lily discovered in western China is so named for its huge white flowers flushed with pink. In China, white lilies represent 100 years of love, symbolizing good luck, and are used in wedding decorations. In some cultures, including in Britain, the while lily is associated with death and mourning, and is frequently included in funeral wreaths.

Iris

A message of beauty and power

In Greek mythology, Iris is a goddess whose name means "rainbow" or "messenger". She travelled the skies as a rainbow that could reach into the sea and the underworld, moving between the worlds of gods and men. Wherever she touched earth, iris flowers bloomed.

Iris also delivered messages and led women from death to the afterlife in the Elysian Fields, a paradise for the immortal. In the hope of gaining Iris's favour for their beloved dead, the ancient Greeks planted irises on graves as offerings.

> " Irises from which
> that rainbow rises "
>
> **Kobayashi Issa**, 1833

The blue *Iris germanica* (bearded iris), found throughout Europe and North Africa, has long been a symbol of life and renewal. It features in the "botanic garden reliefs" at the Temple of Amun-Ra in Karnak, dating from 1500 BCE; an inscription records that all the plants depicted were brought to Egypt from Palestine and Syria. The Egyptians used dried iris roots (underground stems known as rhizomes) in incense and perfume, as did the Romans, who also used them in medicines. The prepared root (orris) is still an ingredient of many perfumes today.

In England, the bearded iris thrived along riverbanks and survived in old gardens and monasteries for centuries. *Culpeper's The Complete Herbal* (1653) lists many medicinal uses for the roots. The juice of the roots was said to ease piles, and a liquor made from them could be gargled to relieve toothache.

Horikiri Iris Garden by Utagawa Hiroshige, 1857

In 19th-century floriography, the meaning ascribed to bearded iris is "flame", perhaps alluding to love or describing the shape of the petals. The fleur-de-lys, based on a stylized iris, was a popular emblem in European heraldry in the 11th and 12th centuries. The banner of the French royal family, for example, features golden fleur-de-lys, said to represent the faith, wisdom, and valour of their sixth-century ancestor Clovis, the first Christian King of the Franks. According to legend, Clovis, trapped between the River Rhine and enemy Goths, noticed yellow flag irises (*Iris pseudacorus*) growing in the middle of the river. Recognizing them as plants that flourish in marshy ground, he guided his army safely across the river, confident that the water would be shallow. Clovis's subsequent success in battle against the Goths then led him to adopt the fleur-de-lys on his coat of arms.

Other kinds of iris include *Iris versicolor*, native to North America, where the rhizomes were once used by members of the Ojibwe tribe as a laxative, and a Japanese flag iris with wavy petals called *Iris ensata*, which is also native to China, Russia, and Korea.

Artists often use irises to signal lost love or sorrow. Early 18th-century painted screens by Japanese artist Ogata Kōrin feature Japanese water irises. Their strong vertical forms look surprisingly modern, but they allude to an ancient story in Japanese literature in which a man composes a poem about lost love when he sees irises growing by a stream. The first syllable of each line forms the word *kakitsubata* – Japanese for iris.

European artists were also inspired by the flower. Impressionist artist Claude Monet, a gardener as well as a painter, was fascinated by their colour and form, and the effect of light on their petals. In the painting *Portrait of Maria Zambaco* (1870) by Pre-Raphaelite artist Edward Burne-Jones, his subject is beautiful yet sad, with blue iris flowers behind her shoulder, symbolizing the sorrow the artist felt at their doomed love affair.

Van Gogh's irises

Dutch artist Vincent Van Gogh found that painting the individual shape of iris flowers calmed him. He completed *Irises*, a painting of bearded irises, shortly after arriving at the St Paul-de-Mausole asylum, a former 12th-century monastery near Arles, where he had voluntarily admitted himself in 1889. The irises that grew in the grounds inspired other iris paintings, including this one (left), in the highly productive period before his death the following year.

> " O! flower-de-luce,
> bloom on, and let the river
> Linger to kiss thy feet! "

Henry Wadsworth Longfellow, "Flower de Luce", 1867

Sweet Pea

◇

Friend and foe

In the late 1690s, Francisco Cupani, a gardener at a monastery in Sicily, noticed a plant whose small maroon coloured flowers had an intense fragrance. It was the sweet pea (*Lathyrus odoratus*), native to the southern tip of Italy and Sicily. Cupani cultivated the plant and later shared the seeds with other botanists, who created plants in a rainbow of colours. By the 19th century, sweet peas were popular across Europe and the US and were often given as thank-you gifts. For this reason, the plant was associated with friendship and goodbyes.

Yet the sweet pea is not the charming but inoffensive plant that many people think. Some species, such as *L. sativus* (also known as Indian pea), which have been used as a source of protein since antiquity, contain a powerful toxin that can cause neurodegenerative disease when consumed over a long period of time. The lathyrus plants were also powerful medicines. The roots of the veiny peavine (*L. venosus*), for example, were used to stop bleeding among several Native American tribes. The Chippewa people credited the plant with magical qualities and carried the root as an amulet to ensure safety and success.

Larkspur

Snub-nosed dolphins

Blooms of larkspur moving in the breeze are sometimes compared to birds or butterflies, but to the ancient Greeks, the bobbing flower buds reminded them of snub-nosed dolphins riding the waves – hence delphinium (from *delphínion*, Greek for dolphin), the plant's other name. In Greek mythology, larkspur was said to have sprung from the spilt blood of either the Spartan prince Hyakinthos, who was killed by a discus (see pages 154–55), or Ajax, hero of the Trojan war, who threw himself upon his own sword. According to Ajax's story, the petals of the larkspur that issued from his blood formed the letters "AI", the first letters of Aias, his name in ancient Greek.

Larkspur has long been present in North America. According to the folklore of the Pawnee people, the flowers were created when a celestial figure cut a hole in the sky to look down on humans, scattering shards of blue sky – larkspur – over the Earth.

Larkspur is poisonous to livestock and humans, although the flowers and root have been used in the past to make a shampoo to eliminate lice and fleas, and the flowers to create a blue dye and ink. In 19th century floriography, blue larkspur represented lightness and levity, while white blooms signified happiness, pink fickleness, and purple haughtiness.

Morning Glory

Symbol of life's brevity

The violet-purple flowers of convolvulus, often known as morning glory, bloom for just one day, unfurling in the early morning and fading away in the afternoon. This brevity accounts for its popular name and has given it a profusion of meanings, including unrequited love, longing, and friendship. Poets and artists sometimes use it as a symbol for the fleeting nature of love and life.

In Japan, morning glory represents the brevity and delicacy of young love and was wildly popular during the Ogosho era (1804–29) of the Edo Period, when many different strains of the flower were cultivated. It often features in art of the period and in haikus (short poems). In China, it symbolizes unrequited or restricted love. According to Chinese legend, there were two lovers who neglected their daily tasks in order to meet. Annoyed by this, the gods separated the lovers by a river, and only allowed them to be together for one day a year. The morning glory's ability to spread across wide, open spaces reminded people of the legend.

> **"** A morning glory at my window satisfies me more than the metaphysics of books. **"**
>
> **Walt Whitman**, *Song of Myself*, 1855

Beauty Standing Beside Morning Glories (c.1814–17), by
Kikukawa Eizan

In the Christian faith, morning glory also represents renewal and
rebirth because, although each flower lasts for only one day, new
flowers appear the following morning. The plant was included in
many 17th-century Dutch still-life paintings for its associations with
Christ's resurrection, often a counterpoint to the other flowers
depicted, whose wilting blooms were intended as a *memento mori* –
a reminder of death's inevitability. In Victorian England, the morning
glory signified unrequited love and extinguished hopes. At the same
time, its blooms and twining tendrils were often carved on Victorian
gravestones to indicate a love that never died.

Old Roses

The statement roses

In the 19th century, many new types of rose – now known collectively as Old Roses – were created across Europe and America. French plant breeders led the way, inspired by the collection created by the Empress Joséphine at the Château de Malmaison near Paris. In 1824, Belgian flower painter Pierre-Joseph Redouté completed a famous set of 117 illustrations of roses at Malmaison and in other French collections. At the same time, roses featured extensively in books on floriography, which were then becoming popular.

To give someone one of these desirable roses was to show admiration for the recipient's beauty or to make an expression of love, but more nuance could be conveyed by the particular type of rose. The damask rose, the best source of rosewater, was said to complement a woman's beautiful complexion or grace. To send a musk rose, with its strong evening fragrance, was bolder, as it was said to represent capricious beauty. A fashionable type, such as a cabbage rose, also known as the centifolia, with full round blooms and a sweet fragrance, was considered an "ambassador of love". Originating in the

" What's in a name?
That which we call a rose
By any other name
would smell as sweet. "

William Shakespeare, *Romeo and Juliet*, 1597

Nineteenth-century
illustration of a tea rose

Netherlands and popular in Europe, it sometimes featured as symbols of beauty in 17th- and 18th-century portraits of aristocratic women. Moss roses, a type of centifolia, symbolized "superior merit", which may have been a way of saying that the recipient was chosen above others, signalling a confession of love.

The appropriate level of affection could be expressed by the colour of the rose, a convention that still holds today. In the 19th century, the choice ranged from white and cream through shades of pink and extending to crimson-purple. The deeper or richer the colour, the more intense the emotion. A white rose meant innocent love; pink, an affectionate or growing love; and purple-red, deep passion. This code was an echo of Greek mythology, in which Chloris, the goddess of flowers, breathed new life into a lifeless nymph in order to turn her into a flower. Chloris then asked each god to add a further gift. Apollo (the sun god) warmed the flower, Aphrodite (the goddess of love) added beauty, and Dionysus (the god of wine) gave a drop of nectar for the flower's fragrance. Finally, the three Graces (the daughters of Zeus) added bloom, more beauty, and joy.

> ❝ The rose looks fair,
> but fairer we it deem
> For that sweet odour
> which doth in it live. ❞

William Shakespeare, *Sonnet 54*

The stages of a bloom were also symbolic. A rose in bud was innocent; a swelling rose offered promise; while one that was open was at the peak of beauty or sexuality. A dried rose implied that love had died, but if the fragrance lingered, it could mean memories of love.

Nineteenth-century poetry and painting also drew on the symbolism of the rose. In Britain, artists of the Pre-Raphaelite Brotherhood (formed in 1848) were well acquainted with flower language, and roses regularly featured in their paintings of women. Dante Gabriel Rossetti included images of full-blown roses in paintings of women at their peak of beauty or sexuality.

As the types of roses and the books on floriography increased, many different and contradictory meanings arose. By the start of the 20th century, the symbolism for roses had become confusing. Modern roses were appearing, beginning a new chapter in the language of flowers (see pages 106–09).

Monna Pamona (1864) by Dante Gabriel Rossetti

Midsummer flowers

During Sweden's Midsummer festival, wildflowers such as roses and daisies are gathered to make a crown, a symbol of rebirth and fertility. As the old Swedish saying "Midsummer night is not long but it sets many cradles to rock" implies, romance is in the air. It is said that an unmarried woman who places seven types of wildflowers under her pillow will dream of her future husband.

Hibiscus

The scarlet messenger

A member of the mallow family with bell-shaped flowers, the hibiscus symbolizes femininity, beauty, and passion. Now unknown in the wild, it was first cultivated in China. The Chinese hibiscus (*Hibiscus rosasinensis*), or China rose, spread through the Pacific region.

In India, the red hibiscus is linked to the Hindu goddess Kali, and red hibiscus garlands are laid in her honour during *puja* – worship of the goddess. According to Hindu mythology, the gods created Kali, representing primordial energy, to help them fight an army of demons. At the end of the battle, which the gods win, Kali continues her dance of destruction across the battlefield until she realizes she has stepped on Shiva, her consort, who is lying on the ground. In shame, Kali stops raging and sticks out her tongue. She is often depicted in this way, her tongue being the symbol of her energy, which is both destructive and life-affirming. The hibiscus flower is said to represent her tongue.

In Hawaii, where the hibiscus is the state flower, young women wear red flowers in their hair – behind the left ear to indicate that they are seeking a lover, behind the right to indicate that they have one already. It is the national flower of Malaysia, where it is known as *bunga raya*, meaning great or celebration flower.

High in antioxidants and vitamin C, dried hibiscus flowers have long been used as a tea. When crushed, the flowers produce a thick, dark secretion that is used in some countries as shoe polish, giving rise to another popular name, the shoe-black flower.

> " I remember the Mother,
> Lustrous as the scarlet hibiscus,
> Her body pasted with saffron and sandal,
> Her hair kissed by musk. "

Hymns to the Goddess

Lotus

Mother of gods

According to fossil records, the lotus plant (*Nelumbo nucifera*) has existed for around 83 million years. Able to survive in extremes of heat and cold, it grows throughout south and southeast Asia, where it is considered a symbol of purity, divinity, and rebirth in both Hinduism and Buddhism.

In India, the lotus grows in rivers and swamps, where it buries its roots in the mud. Its exquisite flower – in shades ranging from white to deep pink – opens to the sun each morning and disappears underwater at night, reappearing next morning unsullied by the murky conditions in which it lives.

> **❝ Varuna, god of the ocean, gave her a divine crest jewel, earrings, bracelets and a garland of unfading lotuses. ❞**
>
> **The Devi Mahatmyam**, *c.* 5h–6th century CE

According to one of the Hindu origin stories, Brahma, the creator of the Universe, sprang from a lotus that flowered from the god Vishnu's navel. Brahma then divided the lotus into three parts – the heavens, the earth, and the sky. In Vedic texts, the sacred literature of Hinduism, dating to 1400 BCE, several gods appear holding or standing on lotus flowers; Lakshmi, goddess of wealth and good fortune, rises from the ocean on a lotus flower, holding two more lotus flowers aloft. And when it comes to humankind, the Vedas describe the heart as having the shape of the lotus, while the body's energies are depicted as lotus flowers. The highest centre of energy, the head, is described as a thousand-petalled lotus flower.

Early Buddhist teachings compared the Buddha to the lotus, the open flower standing above the muddy water symbolizing the divine qualities of detachment and enlightenment. Images of the Buddha often represent him sitting on a lotus flower. According to legend, lotus flowers appeared in his footsteps.

In Victorian England, the lotus flower symbolized estranged love, a meaning that has evolved in modern times into forgetfulness of the past and the making of new beginnings.

Waterlily

The river queen

The waterlily species of North America and Europe are lovers of quiet waters, where their submerged rhizomes, or roots, can lie undisturbed in the mud and produce a profusion of flowers on the surface of the water. Some Native American tribes used to harvest the roots in autumn to use as a medicine. The Mi'kmaq of Canada's Atlantic provinces and northeast Maine, in the US, applied boiled rhizomes as a poultice to reduce swellings. The Ojibwe people of the northeast gargled with a tea made from the roots to relieve coughs. In Europe, 17th-century books on herbs described similar treatments using the European waterlily. Recent research has found that the rhizomes and other parts of the plant have astringent and antiseptic properties.

In the Victorian language of flowers, the American and European waterlily, which have white flowers, represented purity of heart. But the waterlily also had a dark side. In Greek mythology, water nymphs drowned visitors in the lakes and waterways they guarded, and are the source of the plant's scientific name, *Nymphaea*. English painter John William Waterhouse's *Hylas and the Nymphs* (1896) depicts the nymphs as seductive waterlilies in human form, first tempting, then pulling, Hylas, the lover of Heracles, into the water.

> " Like all beautiful people, the waterlilies rise late and even then the sun has to come and beg them. "

Marc Elder, 1924

In the late 19th century, plant breeders introduced waterlilies with pink, red, or yellow flowers. When French nurseryman Joseph Bory Latour-Marliac exhibited the new waterlilies in Paris in 1889, they caught the eye of French Impressionist painter Claude Monet, who later bought some for his Japanese-style water garden at Giverny. Monet was 60 years old when he finished his first Giverny painting of waterlilies and continued to paint them obsessively into his eighties.

One of Claude Monet's waterlily paintings

American Trail Roses

Reminders of courage and resilience

In 1838, the US government forced the Cherokee people to leave their lands in Georgia and nearby states and go to Oklahoma. Gold had been discovered in Georgia, and 7,000 troops were mobilized to remove the Cherokee people, sometimes threatening them with guns. Thousands of Cherokee people died on the 8,120-km- (5,045-mile-) long trails, a journey known as the Trail of Tears.

Among the stories that the Cherokee people tell about this period in their history is the legend of the Cherokee rose – *R. laevigata*. According to the story, the elders were so distressed by the tears of the Cherokee women that they prayed for something to sustain them, so that the children would survive and grow up to rebuild the Cherokee Nation. The following day, looking back along the trail,

> " Where their tears have fallen [will grow] a plant that will have seven leaves for the seven clans of the Cherokee. Amidst the plant will be a delicate white rose with five petals. "

The Legend of the Cherokee Rose

the women saw white roses. It was said that they had sprung from the women's tears and that the golden stamens in their centres symbolized the white man's greed for gold. The plant was strong and thorny, which symbolized the women's resilience.

Other kinds of rose are associated with the white pioneer farming families who drove their wagons from Missouri to Oregon from 1843 onwards. Women took their favourite roses, such as sweetbriar or the Rosa mundi, with them in the hope of planting them in their new gardens. Sadly, with disease rife, women often ended up placing the roses on the graves of the children they buried along the trail.

But the wild roses of North America can also offer hope. In California, the long-forgotten Sonoma rose (*R. spithamea*) was revived by the forest fires of 2020, which cleared the land of fir trees. With space to grow and sunlight, rose roots buried deep in the forest floor came to life and the Sonoma rose flourished once again.

Honeysuckle

The sweet smell of summer

> **"** I sat me down to
> watch upon a bank
> With ivy canopied
> and interwove
> With flaunting honeysuckle. **"**

John Milton, *Comus*, 1637

Once called woodbine, European honeysuckle (*L. periclymenum*) climbs around trees and romps through hedgerows, its nectar-rich flowers attracting bees and other insects. Its entwining tendrils and strong fragrance, especially at night, account for the flower's associations with love. Plants could be trained outside a cottage to indicate marital bliss, and a honeysuckle arbour was ideal for summer evening trysts. The *Honeysuckle Bower* (*c.* 1609) by Flemish artist Paul Rubens shows the artist and his wife sitting hand in hand under honeysuckle.

In China, dreams of honeysuckle indicated passion, while country lore in England advised against taking honeysuckle into the home in case its intoxicating scent aroused female desire. At the same time, young women were told to put a honeysuckle flower under their pillow if they wanted to dream of the man who would be their true love. In the Victorian language of flowers, the honeysuckle came to represent "the bonds of love" and "the generous and devoted affection" of marriage.

Folklore concerning honeysuckle does not only concern love. In Scotland, honeysuckle was traditionally believed to have protective properties. Midwives placed garlands of honeysuckle around women giving birth, and farmers planted it around barns to keep cattle safe and repel evil spirits. In Germany, honeysuckle was traditionally called witch-snare on account of its tenacious stems.

Honeysuckle was well known to Native American people too. The Lakota people sucked the deliciously sweet nectar out of the trumpet of coral honeysuckle (*L. sempervirens*), which grows in the eastern and southern parts of the US. First People have traditionally used juice from chewed leaves to treat bee stings, and created decoctions from boiled leaves to treat coughs and sore throats. In the Victorian flower language, the coral honeysuckle's red-orange flowers represented "the colour of my fate" rather than the intoxication symbolized by the common honeysuckle, perhaps because this flower has no scent.

These days it is Asian honeysuckle (*L. japonica*) that is considered to have medicinal properties. It has multiple uses in Chinese medicine, from treating pneumonia to soothing boils.

Love-in-a-mist

———— ◊ ————

The herb from heaven

An old European legend links this modest flower, popularly known as nigella, to a true event. In 1190, the Holy Roman emperor, Frederick I, drowned in the Saleph river (the Göksu river in Turkey) on his way to lead the Third Crusade, an attempt by European monarchs to reconquer the Holy Land from the Turks. For Frederick's troops, it was an unmitigated disaster, and several legends arose to explain his drowning in the river's shallow waters. According to one tale, a water spirit with long green hair seduced and then drowned Frederick, causing nigella plants to spring up along the riverbank, their wispy foliage suggesting the water spirit's hair.

Originally from Syria, as the botanical name *Nigella damascena* suggests, but native to the wider Mediterranean area and North Africa, the plant's mystical reputation preceded its introduction across Europe in the 16th century. The flower became known as bride-in-hair as brides married with their hair down to signify virginity, and nigella made the perfect flower garland. It was also cultivated for its aromatic seeds.

By the 19th century, the blue flower represented love, and the fringe of soft, fine foliage, the "mist" of its name. When the inflated seed capsules dry out, however, they look like little dark horns, which gave rise to another name, "devil-in-the-bush". No wonder the nigella meant "perplexity" in the Victorian flower language. The seeds of the related *N. sativa*, also known as black cumin, are used in oil, paste, or

> ❝ All day in the sun, when
> the breezes do all they list,
> His soft blue raiment of
> cloudlike blossom abided ... ❞

Algernon Charles Swinburne

powder form in the cuisines of India, Turkey, Iran, Egypt, and Tunisia. They also feature as a traditional medicine in Islamic, Unani, and Ayurveda systems of remedy. Ancient herbalists called the plant "the herb from heaven" because it was an effective treatment for many different conditions, including asthma and headaches. According to the Hadith (sayings of the Prophet), the Prophet Muhammad once stated, "This black cumin is healing for all diseases except death." This made black cumin a "Prophetic medicine" among Muslim people.

Marigold

Sacred flower

For the Aztecs, the native marigold (*Tagetes erecta*), which they called *cempoalxóchitl*, was sacred, because it resembled the sun and was also associated with war, blood, and an honourable death. The Florentine Codex, an account of Aztec culture during the Spanish occupation (1521–1821), records that the plant was cultivated in gardens and orchards, and also grew wild. It also mentions how women made chains of *cempoalxóchitl* for use in ceremonial dances.

The 16th-century Spanish naturalist and physician Francisco Hernández recorded seven varieties of *cempoalxóchitl* flowers in his *Historia de las plantas de Nueva España* (*History of the Plants of New Spain*). He also listed the ailments that they helped treat, ranging from stomach upsets to liver disorders. Petals of *T. lucida,* known as Mexican mint marigold, were thrown in the faces of prisoners intended for human sacrifice because they were thought to have a calming effect.

The Spanish introduced *cempoalxóchitl* to Spain, where it resembled calendula, a native European species used as a pot herb since antiquity. Both plants were laid at shrines to the Virgin Mary, hence the English name marigold (Mary's gold). The Holy Roman Emperor Charles V (1500–58) had found similar-looking flowers in Algeria, which he called *flos Africanus* – African flowers.

In 1500, the Portuguese established a trade route from eastern Brazil to Goa, and marigolds were introduced to south Asia. In the Hindu faith of the region, the yellow and orange colours of the flowers

> ❝ I paint flowers so they will not die. ❞
>
> **Frido Kahlo**, 1946

An illustration of a marigold, Mughal School, 18th century

have a deep spiritual significance as a symbol of surrender to the gods. Known as *genda* – "herb of the sun" – they adorn the doors and windows of homes during Diwali, the Hindu festival celebrating the triumph of good over evil, and particular shades are associated with certain gods. Garlands of yellow *genda*, for example, are offered to the goddess Saraswati on her birthday, while orange garlands represent purifying fire and are offered to the supreme mother goddess Durga to help her combat evil.

During a Hindu wedding ceremony, marigolds are usually included in the *mandap* (flower canopy), a symbol of protection and prosperity under which the bridal couple sit, and in the flower garlands that they exchange. The married couple each have two garlands and by putting one of these around the neck of their partner, bestow half their spiritual force on the other.

> " Youth! Youth! How buoyant
> are thy hopes! They turn,
> Like marigolds, toward the sunny side. "
>
> **Jean Ingelow**, 1863

Guided by the marigold

At the end of October, Mexico celebrates El Día de los Muertos (The Day of the Dead), a two-day festival combining ancient Mesoamerican, Catholic, and Spanish elements, when families welcome the souls of their deceased relatives back from the dead. According to tradition, the gates of heaven open at midnight on 31 October to let the spirits of children rejoin their families on Earth for 24 hours, and at midnight on 1 November, the spirits of adults are allowed to do the same. Marigolds are a symbol of the sun that guides the deceased back to Earth.

Lady Banks's Rose

Old rose from China

Lady Banks's Rose (*Rosa banksiae* 'Alba Plena')

The greatest diversity of wild rose species is found in western China, and the Chinese have been selecting from these for over a thousand years. The species *Rosa banksiae*, an evergreen climbing rose with single white flowers, grows by streams. It is used as a boundary hedge, in traditional medicine, and to decorate mooncakes. Because of its monthly flowering, it symbolizes longevity.

In Chinese gardens, a form with double flowers is popular. Described as being like "double cherry blossom with the scent of violets", it was brought to the West and introduced to Britain in 1807. Named Lady Banks's Rose (*R. banksiae* 'Alba Plena') after the wife of the British botanist Sir Joseph Banks, it proved too delicate to survive the British winters, but a cutting planted in Tombstone, Arizona in 1885 fared much better and is now listed in *Guinness World Records* as the world's largest rose bush at 830 sq m (9,000 sq ft).

Another *R. banskiae* proved more suited to the British climate. The yellow-flowered 'Lutea' was already well-established in Calcutta Botanic Garden when a young gardener called John Parks brought a Lutea to Britain in 1824. The hardiest Banksian rose, it starts flowering two weeks earlier than most roses and its yellow blooms soon graced the warm, dry gardens of the French Riviera, Italy, and southern Spain.

At the same time, Parks brought back another yellow rose, Parks' Yellow China Rose, the last of the "four stud Chinas", four roses that were used by breeders to produce the many varieties of rose grown in Europe today. In Chinese, this rose is *Danhuang Xianshui* ("the light yellow sweet-water rose"). In the West, roses from China were often called tea roses because they had the scent of China tea leaves.

" A little fragrance always clings to the hand that gives the roses. "

Chinese proverb

Tea Tree

—◇—

Australia's natural healer

The tea tree has meant healing and protection ever since the Bundjalung people of Australia's Northern Rivers region discovered its power as a remedy more than 30,000 years ago. The plant inspired the origin story of Eelemani, a young Bundjalung woman who is given special seeds to scatter on a journey across an unknown land. As she throws the seeds, shoots fly towards the sky and tea trees with white paper bark appear. At night, moonlight illuminates the bark, guiding Eelemani home safely.

The tea tree's properties as a natural healer, especially for skin ailments, reside in its leaves and oil. Captain James Cook is believed to have coined the name tea tree after seeing the Bundjalung brewing its leaves for a health-giving drink. The Bundjalung also rubbed crushed leaves on to wounds, burns, and bites, and the oil from pounded leaves was inhaled to treat respiratory ailments. For Bundjalung women, the tea tree is a totem, a cultural symbol of connection to the land. Traditionally, women bathed and gave birth in the dark, tea tree-stained waters of surrounding lakes as part of ceremonial practices that continue to some extent today.

Geraldton Wax Flower

Gem of the outback

Deceptively delicate in appearance, the Geraldton wax flower (*Chamelaucium uncinatum*) is actually robust and long-lasting when cut, its closely bunched clusters of tiny pink and white flowers staying fresh and bright for weeks. Symbolizing enduring love, success, companionship, and patience in a long and happy marriage – the flower is a favourite in bridal bouquets and in centrepieces at wedding feasts. Its stiff shiny leaves and petals produce a sweet fragrance when crushed.

Cultivated as an ornamental garden plant since the early days of European settlement in Australia more than 200 years ago, the shrub takes its name from the Western Australian coastal town of Geraldton. It grows wild in the bush around the town and south to Perth, forming a dense carpet during the wildflower season from late July. Now Australia's number one cut flower export, millions of stems of Geraldton wax flower wing their way around the world every year.

Its fine needle-shaped leaves have been dried, ground, and used as an aromatic herb in cooking and also to flavour botanical gins for many years. However, an expanding market for uniquely Australian flavours has seen plant breeders develop a variety of edible Geraldton wax flower with a citrussy tang that is used to flavour stocks and sauces, and used in stir-fries.

Modern Rose

◇

Sweet valentine

Bred from the late 19th century onwards, modern hybrid tea roses with their urn-like shape and high-centred blooms fit together in the perfect bouquet. A gift of a dozen red roses on St Valentine's Day on 14 February (known as Lovers' Day in some countries) is the ultimate romantic gesture. This association is reflected in the names of rose varieties such as "Wedding Day", "Perpetually Yours", and "All My Love".

> **"** Give me a rose, cool–petaled, virgin white,
> pure as the morning, mystical as night. **"**

Dorothy Parker, 1926

The symbolic meanings of different coloured roses apply as much to modern varieties as to older ones. The darker the colour, the more intense the emotion: white is for innocence, pink for affection, yellow for friendship (having lost its negative Victorian meaning – jealousy), and dark red for romance and deep love. A deep red rose bush is also a symbol of mourning for a true love, while white rose buds represent purity and youth. In Victorian cemeteries in the US and Britain, a broken rosebud stem carved on a headstone symbolizes a girl who has died before growing into a woman.

The number of roses in a bouquet can also be significant. A single long-stemmed rose is a charming gesture expressing love at first sight, and is sometimes given on a first date, while a dozen constitute a serious declaration of love. But the meaning differs according to the country: in Russia, the more roses the better, as long as an odd number is presented, as an even number is associated with death and mourning. In China, 11 red roses express eternal love, while 13 represents a secret crush.

What matters most, many would argue, is not the colour or the number of roses, but the relationship between the giver and the receiver, as illustrated by an old Chinese legend. The story of the blue rose tells of an emperor who, disturbed by his daughter's opposition to marriage, invites potential husbands to vie for her hand. The princess says that she will not accept any suitor unless

" We can complain because rose bushes have thorns, or rejoice because thorns have roses. "

Abraham Lincoln (attributed)

A 19th-century Valentine card reflects a trend for long-stemmed roses.

he presents her with a blue rose. As no one in the land has ever seen such a rose, the challenge seems impossible and only three suitors are bold enough to try: a brave warrior, a wealthy merchant, and a clever judge.

The warrior brings a beautiful sapphire carved in the form of a rose, but the princess rejects it on the grounds that it is not a true flower. The merchant obtains white roses and has them painted blue, but the princess declares that the roses have been stained with poison. The judge commissions an artist to fashion an exquisite glass rose that he then paints blue, but this is also rejected by the princess.

Just as the emperor is about to give up on his mission, something unexpected happens: the princess falls in love with the palace gardener. Realizing that her father will demand that her lover fulfils her impossible condition – the gift of a blue rose – the princess fears that their love will never be accepted. But the gardener assures her that love can find a way. The next day, he introduces himself to the emperor and presents the princess with a beautiful white rose that he has cut from the palace garden. The princess smiles and says that this is exactly the blue rose she had in mind. The court is indignant at this subtle argument, but the emperor wisely points out that the princess set the condition, and it is for her to decide whether it has been fulfilled. The princess marries the one she truly loves.

The "Peace" rose

After World War II, roses became associated with peace and domestic harmony. A house with roses around the door or a bed of hybrid tea roses in a mix of new colours represented the promise of better things to come. A yellow hybrid tea rose bred in France in the 1930s and originally called "Mme A. Meilland" was renamed "Peace" in 1945. In the 1950s and '60s, the Peace rose became the most famous rose in the English-speaking world.

Bottlebrush

Nature's sweet magnet

In the Kimberley region of Western Australia, Aboriginal mythology relates how the Wurulu-Wurulu – mercurial beings who are rarely seen but roam the bush looking for opportunities to create chaos – steal honey from the nests of wild bees, using bottlebrush flowers tied to the ends of sticks to prise it out. Come across an empty bees' nest, it is said, and you know that the Wurulu-Wurulu, who feature in many Aboriginal myths, have been there.

Popularly known as the bottlebrush for its bright red, spiky flowers, which resemble a bottle-cleaning brush, this shrubby tree, a member of the genus *Callistemon*, is native to Australia. In 1789, the English naturalist Joseph Banks introduced a specimen of *Callistemon citrinus* to London's Kew Gardens, having first come across the plant on his voyage to Botany Bay, New South Wales, in 1770. The plant is now naturalized in many parts of the world. Its scientific name, *Callistemon*, comes from *kalli*, the Greek word for beautiful, and *stemon*, meaning stamen, referring to the flower's long red stamens. A dwarf variety is popularly known as the Little John after the nursery rhyme "Little John Bottlejohn" by American writer Laura E. Richards.

The bottlebrush's sweet nectar is a magnet for hummingbirds, bees, butterflies, and other species of birds and insects. Its flowers are used for cooking and in folk medicine, having long formed part of Aboriginal people's diet in the bush, valued for its nectar and its anti-inflammatory and analgesic properties. Today, bottlebrush flowers provide an aromatic, energy-giving tea and can be added to salads and to cooked dishes such as roast meat and sauces, or turned into jellies and jams.

" The upright, conical flowers with which this eccentric looking shrub is thickly covered resemble pretty closely that useful implement of the pantry. "

Godfrey Charles Mundy, 1855

Passion Flower

Beyond compare

In Christian belief, the passion flower represents holy love and religious fervour. When Spanish missionaries came across the flower in South America, they called it *flos passionis* because, to them, it resembled the different aspects of Christ's suffering during the crucifixion: the three styles represent the three nails, the five stamens the five wounds, the corona of thin filaments the crown of thorns, the ten petals the ten true apostles; and the leaves represent the hands and scourges of Christ's persecutors.

In parts of South America and the Caribbean, the passion flower is still known as the Flower of the Five Wounds. In India, the passion flower's different components are linked to characters in the Hindu epic poem *Mahabharata*, and the plant's name is Krishna kamal.

The flower blooms for just three days, which also links it to the three days between Christ's death and resurrection. In Victorian times, the flower sometimes meant mourning for the death of a loved one.

In the southern US, a blue passion flower is known as the maypop or may apple as it has edible yellow fruits that pop when they are squashed. Some Native American tribes cultivated the plant for food and medicinal uses, such as helping to heal wounds and bruises. As a modern herbal remedy, it is said to bring calm and to alleviate anxiety.

" There has fallen a splendid tear
From the passion-flower at the gate. **"**

Alfred Lord Tennyson, "Maud", 1854

Engraving of *Passiflora violacea* – the violet passionflower

Autumn

Myrtle

The victory flower

Myrtle is native to the scrubland of the Mediterranean region and North Africa, where it is valued for its aromatic foliage, scented white flowers, and small black berries. In ancient Greece and Rome, its leaves signified victory in a bloodless battle. They were the "laurels" presented to poets and athletes, and a wedding crown of myrtle symbolized a bride's perceived success in guarding her virginity. A bride would also bathe in water scented with myrtle flowers on her wedding day, because the blooms were associated with Venus, the goddess of love.

In Judaism, myrtle is one of four sacred plants of the Feast of the Tabernacles, and it is used in several rituals. The righteous are encouraged to study how the myrtle spread its fragrance in the world as inspiration for undertaking good works.

Myrtle means "love" in the 19th-century language of flowers, and the plant is symbolic of peace and of marriage. Germany adopted it both as a bridal flower and as an emblem of the country. When Princess Victoria, the eldest daughter of Great Britain's Queen Victoria, married in 1858, the flower was added to the customary orange-blossom bouquet, beginning a tradition that Britain's royal brides still observe today.

Woodblock print by Tanigami Konan, 1917

Fuchsia

Trumpet of the tropics

I n the 1690s, the French monk and botanist Charles Plumier came across bushy plants with clusters of scarlet tubular flowers on the island of Hispaniola (now Haiti and the Dominican Republic). He named the strikingly beautiful plant *Fuchsia triphylla flore coccinea* after the 16th-century German physician and botanist Leonhart Fuchs. It was the first species of fuchsia to be scientifically described.

Fuchsia plants arrived in Britain in the 18th century and were widely cultivated in conservatories and glasshouses. With its rich red-purple colour and elegant hanging blossom, the fuchsia became a symbol for good taste in the Victorian language of flowers. The colour itself became popular in the second half of the 19th century, after a French chemist patented a new red fabric dye that he called *fuchsine*, soon to be renamed magenta.

In the 20th century, fuchsia was a signature colour of the French designer Yves Saint Laurent, who famously used it for his Rouge Pur Couture No. 19 Le Fuchsia lipstick, launched in 1979. At the time, the height of good taste was a pale lip gloss; the brilliant pink of Le Fuchsia was clearly intended to challenge that.

Sunflower

———◇———

The worshipped worshipper

Vase with Fifteen Sunflowers (1888) by Vincent van Gogh

> **❝** I'm painting with the gusto of a *Marseillais* eating bouillabaisse, which won't surprise you when it's a question of painting large Sunflowers. **❞**

Vincent van Gogh, 1888

In 1889, the Dutch artist Vincent van Gogh completed his second series of sunflower paintings – perhaps his best-known works. In the seven paintings, the large group of cut flowers in a vase are depicted at varying stages, from peak bloom to wilting decline. Van Gogh identified closely with the flowers, signing his name on the vase. In a letter to his brother Theo in 1889, he stated that "the sunflower is mine".

Sunflowers (*Helianthus annuus*), which are native to North and Central America, have had a special significance for many cultures and civilizations. Native Americans have long used the plant as a food source, milling the seeds to produce flour, or roasting them for a snack, and extracting oil from the seeds for cooking. The Paiute of Nevada used a decoction of roots to ease rheumatism, and the Zuni of New Mexico still use fresh or dried roots to treat snakebites.

To the Aztecs, the sunflower was a symbol of the sun and of war. Its flower appears on the shields of several Aztec deities, and the Nahua, descendants of the Aztecs, still refer to the flowers as *chimalacatl*, meaning shield-reed, and *chimalxochitl*, meaning shield-flower. In the 16th century, a Spanish study of Aztec culture known as the Florentine Codex recorded rituals involving the sunflower, including its use in lavish banquets given for visiting guests. It notes how, after inviting their guests to smoke tobacco, their hosts would approach them with a sunflower in their right hand and another flower in their left. Only after these had been accepted by the guests – who took them in the opposite hand – would the food be served.

The Codex also describes offerings of sunflowers and tobacco made at the pyramid of the war god Huitzilopochtli. People burned the tobacco overnight and then buried the ash with offerings to the accompaniment of prayers.

" Light-enchanted sunflower, thou
Who gazest ever true and tender
On the sun's revolving splendour. "

Pedro de Calderón de la Barca, *El mágico prodigioso*, 1637

The Spanish took the sunflower back to Europe in the early 16th century, where it became popular as an ornamental plant. At the turn of the 19th century, it arrived in Russia, where it became an important food source. At the time, the Russian Orthodox Church forbade the consumption of butter and lard during Lent, but did not prohibit the use of sunflower oil.

In 19th-century Europe, the sunflower replaced the heliotrope in the Greek myth of Helios and Clytie. According to the original tale in Ovid's *Metamorphoses*, a water nymph called Clytie was in love with the sun god Helios, but he loved a beautiful girl called Leucothoe. When Helios scorned Clytie, she sat on a rock for nine days, not eating or drinking, only looking at Helios as he passed overhead. Eventually, she wasted away and turned into a pale flower – the European heliotrope – that turns to follow the sun across the sky. The fact that the sunflower also follows the movement of the sun caught people's imagination, and Clytie became a blazing sunflower instead.

In Victorian floriography, the sunflower was a symbol for adoration, though taller sunflowers were said to represent haughtiness. In the 20th century, the flower gained a new meaning when Ukraine became a non-nuclear state following its separation from Russia. In 1996, government ministers planted sunflower seeds – the country's national flower – at the Pervomaysk missile base as a symbol of peace. Subsequently, the flower has been adopted as an international emblem for a world free of nuclear weapons.

Sunflowers and the decorative arts

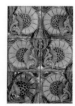

Sunflowers have long fascinated and inspired artists and artisans. Designers in the Arts and Crafts movement of the late 19th century incorporated stylized sunflowers into designs for a wide range of products, including stained glass, wallpaper, textiles, and wrought ironwork. The British artist-potter William De Morgan's sunflower tiles (left), which were often set into fireplaces, were in production for nearly 30 years.

Botanical print of
Acanthus spinosus

Acanthus

Immortal inspiration

The tall flower spikes and thistle-like foliage of *Acanthus spinosus* inspired the Corinthian column, the classical pillar in ancient Greek and Roman architecture. How this came about is related in *The Ten Books on Architecture* by the first-century CE architect Vitruvius.

According to Virtuvius, a freeborn maiden of Corinth, just of marriageable age, became ill and passed away. After her burial, her nurse collected a few things that had given the girl pleasure, put them into a basket and laid it on top of her tomb, covering the top with a roof-tile. This basket happened to be placed just above the root of an acanthus plant. When spring came, the sturdy root produced leaves and stalks, and the stalks grew up around the sides of the basket, pressed out by the corners of the tile. When the architect Callimachus then passed the tomb, he observed the leaves growing around the basket and was inspired to build a new style of column.

The Corinthian column, with its acanthus motif, is the most ornate of the three styles of Greek column. In Mediterranean countries, acanthus came to symbolize long life and immortality.

Yarrow

Trojan medicine

Yarrow, a herb of sunny wastelands, pastures, and meadows, has long been known to have anti-inflammatory and anti-allergenic properties. It has been used throughout the northern hemisphere to accelerate the healing of wounds and as a tea for colds and fevers since ancient times. Among Native American tribes, the Navajo people of the soutwest chewed yarrow to alleviate toothache, and the Iroquois-speaking Haudenosaunee of the northeast used it to treat convulsions and fevers in children.

Mindful of the plant's healing properties, the 18th-century Swedish botanist and taxonomist Carl Linnaeus assigned yarrow the scientific name *Achillea millefolium* in honour of the Greek mythological hero Achilles, who carried the herb with him during the Trojan War to stanch his men's wounds. According to the myth, Achilles acted on the advice of his mentor, the centaur physician Chiron, himself an expert healer.

This Classical reference accounts for yarrow's meanings in the 19th-century floriography – war, courage, and good health. Other common names for yarrow include allheal, soldier's woundwort, and "the military herb".

In the Middle East, yarrow is taken as a tea to ease abdominal problems. In Ayurvedic medicine, it is mixed with sage and used as a tonic for the nervous system. In Britain, dried yarrow with elderflower and peppermint used to be a common country remedy for colds and flu.

Agapanthus

⊷ ✣ ⊶

Phoenix of the fynbos

A plant of the fynbos – the natural shrubland of South Africa's Western and Eastern Cape provinces – agapanthus (*A. Africanus*) has a long history as a traditional remedy and talisman among the Indigenous people of the country. Xhosa brides wear a necklace made from agapanthus roots as a lucky charm, in the hope it will ensure an abundance of children and easy childbirth. Young mothers caring for their first child wear a similar necklace to ensure health and happiness for them both. Decoctions of the rhizome (underground stem) and roots are used in prenatal care; or sometimes a plant may be grown in water and the water – known as *isihlambezo* in Zulu and *isicakathi* in Xhosa – is drunk instead. The strap-like leaves are used externally to soothe sore and tired feet, and may be wound around wrists to bring down fevers, but they are never ingested.

In the wild, agapanthus grows between rocks on east-facing mountain slopes. Fire is a natural feature of the highly flammable fynbos habitat, and agapanthus not only survives its occurrence but flowers more profusely afterwards. Blue, purple, or occasionally white flowers grow in umbels – bunch formations – from a single stem; below ground, its thick rhizome produces a tangle of roots, which help it survive the hot, dry summers.

The Dutch took agapanthus plants from South Africa to the Netherlands, where one specimen flowered in 1679. Eventually, the plant, which blooms profusely when pot-bound, became a popular feature in conservatories all over Europe. The genus name, *Agapanthus*, comes from the Greek words *agapē* meaning love and *anthos* meaning flower – flower of love – possibly because parts of the plant were reputedly used as an aphrodisiac in Africa.

Agapanthus by British botanical illustrator Walter Hood Fitch (1817–92)

<blockquote>

❝ The more I am confined,
the more I flower. ❞

Dr Craig Wright, *The Fynbos Physician*, 2015

</blockquote>

Loves-lies-bleeding

An Aztec jewel

Love-lies-bleeding (*Amaranthus caudatus*) is named for its long, red, pendulous flowerheads resembling cascades of red tassels. It may have acquired its popular name as early as the 1660s, soon after its introduction into North America and Europe. The species name amaranthus comes from the Greek *amarantos*, meaning unfading flower because the tassels keep their colour as they die.

Native to Central and South America, the plant has been cultivated for more than 4,000 years for ceremonial use and as a food crop. The Aztecs knew it as *huauhtli*. To celebrate the festival of the god Huitzilopochtli, they mixed amaranthus seeds with honey and moulded little figures of the god, which they then cut into small pieces and ate. The Spanish conquerors tried to ban the amaranthus plant, but without success. The seeds are still sometimes used in Mexico, in cooking or ground to produce flour.

Because love-lies-bleeding retains its beauty even after it has died, in the Victorian era, it came to represent both unfading or undying love and immortality. It also became a funerary flower, symbolizing death. The smaller, more upright, purple amaranthus represented hopeless love.

The amaranth of European poetry refers to a different but related species, celosia, which has upright spiky flowers in a variety of colours. According to Greek mythology, the hero Achilles was mourned with wreaths of amaranth, representing immortality; in John Milton's *Paradise Lost*, the amaranth was removed from the Garden of Eden and taken to heaven, where it bloomed eternally.

> " The red flowers hang in pendant spikes, and at a little distance, look like streams of blood. "
>
> **Joseph Banks**

127

Chrysanthemum

◇

The emperor's emblem

Happiness, motherhood, friendship, long life, and death are just some of the often-contradictory meanings of chrysanthemums. In a further complication, the flower's colours have a plethora of meanings around the world – from yellow for longevity to violet for recovery and white for death.

Ancient Chinese scrolls from the 15th century BCE include descriptions of the chrysanthemum. Beautiful and beneficial, it was used as a herbal remedy; the boiled roots were said to relieve headaches and the bloom to balance heat within the body. It has culinary uses too, and is eaten in salads, brewed as a tea, and made into wine. Blooming even in the chill winds of autumn, it signifies the triumph of strength over adversity.

Buddhist monks brought chrysanthemums with them to Japan around the 8th century CE, and the Japanese took the flower to their hearts. Poets wrote about it, artists painted it, healers prescribed it,

> **"** If you would be happy for a lifetime, grow chrysanthemums. **"**
>
> **Chinese saying**

AUTUMN

and members of the court praised its beauty. In the 12th century, Emperor Go-Toba made the flower his emblem, and it later became associated with the nation itself. Japanese passports sport a stylized 16-petalled chrysanthemum and it appears on the 50-yen coin, above the doors of embassies, and stamped on official papers.

Both China and Japan celebrate the flower at the Double Ninth Festival, held on the ninth day of the ninth month (9 September).

" Chrysanthemums ... are like lions. Kingly characters, I always expect them to spring. To turn on me with a growl and a roar. "

Truman Capote, *A Christmas Memory*, 1956

Chrysanthemum, by Piet Mondrian, 1906

At this time, it is traditional to drink chrysanthemum wine and admire the flowers. Chrysanthemum Day is known as the Feast of Happiness in Japan. In 1878, Emperor Meiji invited courtiers to mark the day by visiting his garden to admire chrysanthemums, starting an annual chrysanthemum flower show where growers vie to create ever more beautiful and exotic varieties (see below). But beware when giving chrysanthemums as a gift: colour matters. In Japan, yellow is associated with the emperor, red chrysanthemums are given as a sign of love and respect, but white blooms are only for funerals, because white is associated with death.

The plant reached Europe in the 17th century, where Swedish botanist Carl Linnaeus gave it the name chrysanthemum, combining two Greek words – *chrysos* meaning golden and *anthemon* meaning flower. In the 19th century, the plant increased in popularity with new varieties being cultivated or brought from China and Japan.

The flower is associated with death in Austria, France, and Belgium, where people place pots of chrysanthemums on the graves of loved ones. In Britain, however, the plants signified friendship and well-wishing in the Victorian language of flowers, while violet blooms brought a get well message.

In North America, the chrysanthemums' cheery autumnal colours, which range from pale yellow to golden orange to darkest crimson, brighten front porches, parks, and paths before winter. On the other side of the world Australians celebrate Mother's Day in May, their autumn, with the aptly named "mums".

The changing face of "mums"

Originally a small daisy-like flower, the chrysanthemum is a member of the Compositae family. Over the centuries, plant lovers have created hundreds of varieties. In Japan, growers have created four types: *zukuri* (thousand bloom), *ogiku* (single stem), *kengai* (cascade), and *shino-tsukuri* (driving rain). Skilled growers can train them into a shape that resembles a bonsai tree (right). They have even been bred to have different colours on the face and reverse of the florets.

Aster

Autumn star

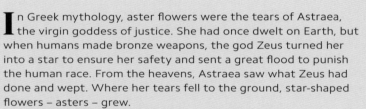

In Greek mythology, aster flowers were the tears of Astraea, the virgin goddess of justice. She had once dwelt on Earth, but when humans made bronze weapons, the god Zeus turned her into a star to ensure her safety and sent a great flood to punish the human race. From the heavens, Astraea saw what Zeus had done and wept. Where her tears fell to the ground, star-shaped flowers – asters – grew.

In North America, a Cherokee legend tells of two sisters who ran away when their fellow villagers were slain by a rival tribe. Far away, a woman with magical powers foresaw that the sisters would be hunted down, so turned them into flowers while they slept under the stars. One sister became the lavender-blue aster, the fringe of her dress its outer petals; the other sister became the yellow goldenrod.

The Okanagan-Colville people of British Columbia and Washington state used the root of the aster *Eurybia conspicua* as a remedy for toothache. But the main medicinal aster is the Asian species, *Aster tataricus*, which is used to treat chest infections.

Asters in a Vase (1875) by Henri Fantin-Latour

" The aster greets us as we pass
with her faint smile. **"**

Sarah Helen Whitman, 1853

In 19th-century floriography, asters coveyed a farewell, and China
asters (*Callistephus chinensis*) meant, "I partake in your sentiments."
Asters are also known as Michaelmas daisies as they flower on
St Michael's Day (29 September) a time of harvest festivals.

Botanical print
of rudbeckia –
black-eyed Susan

Black–eyed Susan

Fields of red and gold

Popularly known as black-eyed Susan, rudbeckia fills North American waysides and wild-flower meadows with patches of brilliant colour, a cheering sight that led to it becoming Maryland's state flower in 1918. For Native Americans who occupied these landscapes for thousands of years, the plant was invaluable as a remedy for swellings, sores, burns, earache, and snake bites. South and west of the Great Lakes, the Potawatomi and Menominee people cooked the tender spring leaves as health-giving vegetables.

With its dark central cone surrounded by yellow petals, rudbeckia came to be known as black-eyed Susan after a popular song of that name (about a young woman and her sailor lover, Sweet William), introduced by colonists in the 18th century. In the 19th century the plant inspired the look of one of American designer Louis Comfort Tiffany's famous series of art nouveau lamps.

Coneflower

Healer of the prairies

For the people of the Great Plains of central and eastern North America, the bright-coloured flowerheads of echinacea – or coneflower – had a multitude of medicinal uses. The Cheyenne brewed a tea from the plant to treat rheumatism and arthritis; the Blackfoot and Lakota people chewed its roots as a painkiller; and warriors of the Hidatsa nation nibbled the roots to give them energy on a long journey and also chewed them in sweat lodge rituals to purify the body and soul. The Ute people believed that wounded elk sought out echinacea plants for their healing properties and called them "elk flower". The Kiowa tribe chewed the roots when they had colds and used the dried seed heads to comb their hair.

In the 17th century, European colonists in America embraced echinacea as a cold remedy and sent specimens back to Europe, where the 18th-century German botanist Conrad Moench later coined the scientific name *Echinacea*, from the Greek word *ekhinos*, meaning "hedgehog" or "sea urchin", a reference to the spiny seed heads.

The medicinal reputation of echinacea is still strong. *E. purpurea* and *E.angustifolia* are sold as dietary supplements, reputed to boost the immune system, though no clear evidence has so far emerged to support this claim.

Hydrangea

•————————•————————•

The changeling

Hydrangeas by Agnes Goodsir (1864–1939)

In the wild, the Japanese hydrangea (*Hydrangea macrophylla*) grows in woodlands. During Japan's Edo period (1600–1868), the Samurai regarded its changeable colour (blue flowers sometimes turn pink) as a symbol of infidelity. Later, however, it lost this association and was often planted in temple gardens. Today, statues of the Buddha are anointed with hydrangea tea on the Buddha's birthday. This is made from young leaves that have been fermented to reduce their toxicity.

In Japan, the plant is known as *ajisai*, possibly derived from *azusai*, meaning "gathering of blues", an allusion to the blue flowers that come with the rainy season. In haiku poetry, the combination of blue flowers and rain symbolizes melancholy. When the plant arrived in Europe, blue was regarded as a cold colour, hence the 19th-century floriography meaning, "you are cold". Yet pink blooms, which were originally called Hortensia, could refer to a cheerful woman.

The hydrangea also conveys "gratitude for being understood", a meaning derived from a true story about 19th-century German military physician and botanist Philipp von Siebold. Posted to Japan, Siebold lived for several years with a Japanese woman named Kusumoto Taki, whom he called Otakusa. In 1829, Siebold was expelled for having secret maps of the country and left Otakusa behind. In his book *Flora Japonica*, published in 1835, he immortalized his former lover by naming a species of hydrangea *H. otaksa*.

" Hydrangea! In a grove,
a little garden, the detached room. "

Matsuo Bashō, 1694

Saffron Crocus

Culinary gold

The saffron crocus (*Crocus sativus*) was first grown as a field crop in Crete around 700 BCE. An ancient Greek myth tells how the mortal youth Krokos, beloved by the god Hermes, was transformed into the saffron flower by the Greek god after he had been struck on the head and killed. According to the story, the red stigma are drops of Krokos's blood.

All crocus flowers have a stigma, but in *C. sativus* it is long and hangs down between the petals. When the stigma is picked and dried, its strands or filaments become saffron, the highly valuable spice. After the 11th century, several places in Europe and the Middle East specialized in the production of saffron, though today *C. sativus* is mostly grown in Iran. The flowers are harvested early in the morning and then taken indoors, where the stigma is picked out by hand.

> **"** Saffron is a herb of the Sun, and under the Lion, and therefore you need not a reason why it strengthens the heart. **"**

Nicholas Culpeper, *The Complete Herbal*, 1653

Woman picking saffron, medieval manuscript illustration

In ancient Greece, saffron was harvested to make royal dyes and perfumes, but in India and China it acquired new meanings and uses. The saffron flag, with its two triangles, is a symbol of sacrifice and identifies Hindi temples and kingdoms. Saffron is used to dye the robes of Buddhist monks and to mark a *bindi* – a third eye symbolizing good fortune and conscience – on a Hindu woman's forehead.

The Chinese have long used saffron to treat depression, and the Victorian flower meaning of "mirth" stemmed from this, although the right dose was vital. According to an English proverb, "Saffron makes you laugh, but too much of it will make you laugh yourself to death."

Panier de Dahlias
(1893) by Henri
Fantin-Latour

Dahlia

The jewel flower

Central America is the home of the wild species of dahlia. In August and September, when the rainy season is over, the highlands around Mexico City are ablaze with the flowers. They were used as a food source by the Aztecs, but unlike marigolds and sunflowers, there is little evidence that they were of symbolic importance to them.

The Spanish took dahlias to Europe at the end of the 18th century, and by the early 19th century there were dahlias in many colours as well as plants with double flowers growing on the continent. The spiky-petalled *Dahlia juarezii* created great excitement when it was listed for sale in the Netherlands in 1874.

One of the first dahlias taken to Europe was *D. pinnata*, which is still harvested as a wild or home-grown plant for dye (from the flowers and seeds) and for food. All parts of dahlias are edible. Their petals, fresh or cooked, add colour to salads or cooked snacks, while the tubers can be eaten raw but are mostly cooked then peeled. In Central America, the tubers are boiled as a vegetable, and the cooking liquid used in drinks. A sweet extract from roasted tubers, called *dacopa*, adds a mocha-like flavour to food and drinks.

" September is dressing herself
in a show of dahlias and splendid
marigolds and starry zinnias. "

Oliver Wendell Holmes, 1862

DAHLIA

Aconitum

❦

The hooded claw

Botanical illustration of *Aconitum lycoctonum*, 1820

❝ It's probably the most poisonous plant that people will have in their garden. ❞

John Robertson, 2014

With poisonous roots and hooded purple flowers, aconitums are the stuff of dark myths and folklore. According to Greek mythology, one of the 12 labours of Heracles was to fetch Cerberus, the three-headed hound of Hades, from underground. When the beast appeared, its spittle dripped on the Earth, and up sprang the first aconites. Other myths that feature aconites include one about the goddess Athene, who sprinkles the maiden Arachne with aconite juice and turns her into a spider, and one about the sorceress Medea, who attempts to poison Theseus with wine laced with aconite juice to prevent him from displacing her son in the line of succession.

Swedish botanist and taxonomist Carl Linnaeus named a yellow-flowered species *Aconitum lycoctonum* subsp. *vulparia* – *lycoctonum vulparia* meaning "wolf-slaying". Hunters applied the highly poisonous plant to arrows when hunting wolves, hence its common name of wolfsbane.

A. napellus, which was once used by apothecaries, is known as monkshood because of the shape of its purple-blue flowers. These also resemble a knight's helmet, hence its Victorian flower meaning – chivalry. All species of aconitum are extremely poisonous.

Zinnia

Prairie bloom

The zinnia of the southwestern US and Mexico, often known as the Plains or Rocky Mountains zinnia, cover the ground in a carpet of flowers. In Navajo mythology, zinnia symbolizes the Ever-changing Woman, the goddess who grew old and then became young again because, as the petals of the flower age, new young florets appear at its centre. It was a sacred plant with medicinal uses, and was also used to make dyes for body paint. To some Pueblo tribes, it signified wisdom.

According to a Navajo legend, when the tribe's corn crops kept failing and it was threatened with famine, a young boy was sent to find Spider Woman, the weaver of the Universe and helper of humans. As he searched for her, yellow zinnias sprouted in his footsteps. The Spider Woman's advice was to gather up the zinnia flowers and plant them in the fields. It turns out that zinnias attract a type of bug that eats the mites that feed on corn plants.

The first Europeans to come across zinnia were the Spanish in Mexico in the 1520s. They called it *mal de ojos* (sickness of the eye). In 19th-century America, the flower was referred to as "youth in old age", echoing the older association with the Ever-changing Woman. In the Victorian language of flowers, zinnias were reserved for friends, and the red zinnia stood for remembrance.

ZINNIA

" I pluck the flower one moment to behold
   Its treasury of purple and of gold. "

Anonymous

Leucadendron

◆

Firecracker of the Cape

Carl Linnaeus, the father of modern taxonomy, named the Protea family after Proteus, an early sea-god in Greek mythology, because the flowers were "greatly variable and different like Proteus himself". Proteus could see the future and always spoke the truth, but to extract a prophecy, the seeker had to grasp him tightly while he changed into various beasts, and then into fire and water.

The Protea family contains a wide range of flowering plants, including the leucadendron, or conebush. Most leucadendrons are shrubby evergreens, which grow on the rocky hills and slopes of South Africa's Cape, surviving on nutrient-poor soils and

> **"** The most shining and splendid of all plants. **"**

Carl Linnaeus

dependent on the 10–15-year cycle of natural fires that create enough heat to crack open the plant's seedheads. Their bright red or yellow bracts surrounding the yellow-green flowerheads add colour to the Cape's shrubland. On the other hand, the endangered *Leucadendron argenteum*, or silver tree, is named for its gleaming metallic lustre.

Other proteas of South Africa include *Protea nitida*, known as the wagon tree by Afrikaner settlers in the early 1800s. They used its wood for making wagon-wheel rims and tobacco pipes, and its bark for tanning leather. They also collected nectar from the flowerheads of the sugarbush (*P. repens*) to make a syrup known as *bossiestroop*, which they used to soothe coughs and as a sweetener.

In the 19th century, proteas were grown successfully in heated glasshouses in Europe, and they were soon given meanings – "transformation" and "courage" – in the Victorian language of flowers. In South Africa, however, it was only after Kirstenbosch National Botanic Garden near Cape Town started displaying proteas in 1920 that their beauty was fully accepted. Now, South Africans often give cut proteas as gifts.

Periwinkle

Love's restraint

66 The leaves, eaten together
by man and wife, caused
love between them. 99

Nicholas Culpeper, *The Complete Herbal*, 1653

It used to be said that periwinkle or vinca – from the Latin *vinicio*, meaning "to bind or restrain", a reference to the plant's trailing stems – was used by Cupid to bind lovers together. For the 18th-century Swiss philosopher Jean-Jacques Rousseau, the flower was a bringer of happy memories. Spotting a periwinkle beside a path while out walking one day, he was flooded by memories of his romance, 30 years previously, with Françoise-Louise de Warens. She had pointed out just such a periwinkle flower on the first day of their affair.

Vinca species are native to Europe, North Africa, and the Middle East. In medieval Europe, periwinkle was believed to be an aphrodisiac and a remedy against diseases both spiritual and physical.

"This wort is of good advantage … against devil sickness and demoniacal possession", notes one monastic herbal. Periwinkle was also used to treat nosebleeds. In Ukraine, it was laid around a baby's cradle to protect the baby while it slept. In Italy, it was planted on the graves of those who had died in infancy.

The leaves, seeds, flowers, and roots of the pink-flowered Madagascar periwinkle (*Catharanthus roseus*) are used in Ayurvedic medicine to help treat diabetes and cancer. The plant's medicinal properties are attested by modern science. Chemicals, known as vinca alkaloids, first identified in the plant's leaves and now produced synthetically, are used to treat Hodgkin's disease and leukaemia.

Crinum Lily

❖

The sleeping beauty

Most wild crinums come from tropical southern Africa. A favourite for traditional medicine, *C. bulbispermum* lives in the mud bed of the Gariep river, between Namibia and South Africa. Thanks to its large bulb – sometimes weighing several kilograms – the plant can stay dormant for long periods in baked mud. Then, when the river fills up, it bursts into life, producing beautiful perfumed flowers.

The Sotho people of Lesotho and South Africa make a strong brew from the leaves and crushed bulbs of the crinum lily to treat colds and coughs. The Zulu and Tswana people use the plant to relieve swelling or pain in joints or backache; they bind flowers or pieces of roasted bulb to the affected area using its strap-like leaves as a dressing.

> **"** Crinum ... is spread round, the whole belt of the globe. **"**
>
> **William Herbert**, 1836

Seeds were taken across the Atlantic by enslaved people, and crinum lilies are found growing along many former slave-trading routes. It thrives in the warm southern states of the US, either on riverbanks, abandoned plantations, or in overgrown cemeteries, hence its common name, cemetery lily. Left undisturbed, the bulb grows to a huge size and sustains the plant in periods of drought, just as it does in the dried-up river bed of the Gariep.

Nineteenth-century botanical illustration of a crinum lily

The classic milk-and-wine lily, named for its maroon and white stripes, is *C. x herbertii*, a hybrid produced by British botanist and clergyman William Herbert in 1819. Herbert crossed *C. bulbispermum* with one that tolerates colder temperatures. Popular on old homesteads and gardens in southern Africa and the US for its fragrant flowers, the milk-and-wine lily is notoriously tough: specimens known to have been planted a century ago can still flourish. Today, crinums of all types are experiencing a revival, both as heirloom garden flowers and as a source of new medicines.

CRINUM LILY

Winter

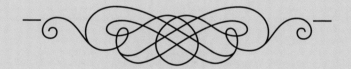

Hyacinth

Heaven's scent

❝ Here hyacinths of heavenly blue,
shook their rich tresses to the morn. **❞**

James Montgomery, 1827

According to Greek myth, Hyakinthos was a handsome young mortal loved by the god Apollo. The pair were playing games one day when a discus struck Hyakinthos a fatal blow to the head. As he lay dying, Apollo caused flowers to spring from his spilt blood. Based on the myth, the Victorian flower meaning for most hyacinths was sport or play, while white hyacinths meant innocence. Some researchers now think that the myth may have referred to larkspur (see page 79), and that the hyacinth is not the ancient Greek flower hyakinthos.

The true hyacinth is *Hyacinthus orientalis*, a bulb native to the eastern Mediterranean and Middle East. The species has fragrant flowers, usually pale blue but sometimes white. Ottoman sultans filled their gardens with hyacinths as well as tulips. On the death of Sultan Murad III in 1595, his son had half a million hyacinth bulbs planted. Still loved in the Middle East, hyacinths are popular decorations for the table at Iranian New Year in March – the flowers and fragrance being potent reminders to celebrate the first day of spring.

Once hyacinths reached Europe in the 16th century, growers expanded the colour range to include darker blue, pink, and purple flowers. Double flowers appeared in 1612, and were popular until the 1850s. Europeans found ways to enjoy the colourful fragrant flowers as indoor plants in winter. In the 18th century, Madame de Pompadour, a mistress of Louis XV of France, created a fashion for growing a hyacinth bulb in a glass of water for display in the Palace of Versailles.

In Germany, England, and Scotland, the woodland bluebell (*Hyacinthoides*), or wild hyacinth, features in folklore. Parents would warn children about fairies who might lure them into the woods with the sound of bells. If they followed them, it was said, they would never be seen again.

HYACINTH

Lily of the Valley

Belle of the ball

According to European folklore, the nightingale loves lily of the valley (*Convallaria majalis*). It is said that the bird will not return to the woods after winter until the lily of the valley blooms in May, symbolizing the return of happiness.

In pagan mythology, the flower is associated with Ostara, the Celtic goddess of spring. The white, fragrant bells symbolize her humility and purity. Among Christians, the flowers were known as Our Lady's tears as they were said to have sprung from the tears shed by the Virgin Mary at the crucifixion of Jesus.

A sixth-century French legend tells of St Leonard, who wanted to live in the woods as a hermit so he could be closer to God. A fire-breathing dragon named Temptation also lived there, and the two of them had many bloody battles. Eventually, St Leonard drove Temptation away. Where the dragon's blood had been spilled, poisonous weeds began to grow; where St Leonard's blood was spilled, beds of lily of the valley appeared.

The practice of forcing scented flowers to bloom extra early so they can be enjoyed over the winter months was popular in 19th-century Europe and North America. This provided a ready supply of lily of the valley for indoor display in a pot or to wear as a buttonhole or corsage at a New Year's Eve ball.

Echo and Narcissus (1903) by British artist John William Waterhouse

Paperwhite

Wedded to a myth

The fragrance of *Narcissus papyraceus* (paperwhite) is the most intense of all the *Narcissus* species. The flower was thought by the ancient Greeks to have narcotic properties and has long been linked to the mythical youth – Narcissus – who rejected the nymph Echo because he was in love with his own reflection, which he had glimpsed in a pool. When the youth pines away and dies for love of himself, a flower – the narcissus – blooms in his place.

Wild paperwhites hail from the warm stony soils of Algeria and Morocco, but they also grow in southern parts of Spain, France, Italy, and Greece, often in rough grass between olive trees. In colder climates, they are grown indoors in pots to brighten up the winter months. In the southern US and California, they are often planted outdoors as an alternative to daffodils, as their bulbs cope better with summer heat.

In China, paperwhites are grown indoors during the winter and timed to flower for the Chinese New Year. The flowers are said to bring good luck and prosperity, especially if they bloom on the first day of the Chinese New Year.

Holly

For protection and winter cheer

Since ancient times, the holly has been the plant of midwinter. In many parts of Europe, it is the most common native evergreen. In wide open winter landscapes, where other trees and plants appear stark and leafless, it is the holly's dark glossy leaves and bright red berries that stand out. Symbolic meanings are often attributed to the plant: the leaves are a sign that growth will return in spring while the red berries stand for menstrual blood and fertility.

In ancient Rome, people exchanged holly wreaths as good luck gifts on the winter feast of Saturnalia, honouring Saturn, the Roman god of sowing. Among Europe's pre-Christian Celtic cultures, the druids considered the holly "king of winter", whose rule reached its peak on the winter solstice. They did not fell these sacred trees, but only cut the branches to hang indoors as a symbol of eternal life during the long dark winter months. Nordic people planted holly trees near their homes to appease the god of thunder.

With the spread of Christianity, holly was banned from churches on account of its pagan associations, but many people continued to hang up holly at home as protection against misfortune. Over time, this was absorbed into Christian tradition, and holly acquired a Christian symbolism: the prickly leaves represented Christ's crown of thorns and the berries his blood. At the same time, holly retained its midwinter associations, and it is now familiar in Christmas wreaths and decorations.

In other parts of the world, other holly species had their own significance. In South America, the Guaraní people in today's Paraguay cultivated *Ilex paraguariensis* to make *yerba mate*, a kind

In the image: *The Merry Heart that keeps afar all care be yours this Christmas*

CHRISTMAS GREETINGS

A Victorian Christmas card captures the festive associations of holly.

of tea, from its leaves. In North America, some Native American tribes used the bark and leaves of *I.opaca* medicinally. The Catawba people, in the Carolinas, created an infusion of the leaves to help relieve the symptoms of measles.

Traditionally, wisdom and foresight is attributed to holly because the quantity of berries, which are an important food source for birds in winter, varies from year to year. According to country lore, a bumper crop of berries signifies that a harsh winter is coming.

> " Be merry all, be merry all,
> With holly dress the festive hall;
> Prepare the song, the feast, the ball,
> To welcome merry Christmas. "

William Robert Spencer, 1835

Ivy

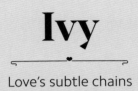

Love's subtle chains

The ivy plant has flourished in Europe for millennia. It was associated with fertility and revelry in pre-Christian times and faithfulness and enduring love in the Victorian era.

Ivy was the symbol of Dionysus, the god of wine in ancient Greece, and of his counterpart, Bacchus, in ancient Rome, both of whom were often depicted wearing a wreath of ivy. Revellers made wreaths and garlands from ivy and other greenery to celebrate the Roman festival of Saturnalia and other midwinter celebrations. The practice persisted into the Christian era, when these pagan festivals were replaced by Christmas. By medieval times, ivy had come to symbolize the Virgin Mary and was combined with holly, representing Jesus Christ (see page 158) to decorate churches at Christmas.

To the Celts, ivy's tenacious ability to bind itself around plants and other items represented determination. Later, the plant came to symbolize faithfulness and endurance in love and friendship. In Britain, a Cornish legend tells of the doomed love affair between Tristan, a local sailor, and Isolde, the bride-to-be of the king of Cornwall. On their deaths, the king had the lovers buried far apart, but it was said that ivy shoots appeared on their graves and grew towards each other, eventually becoming tightly entwined.

In Victorian times, people gave brooches decorated with an ivy leaf motif, signifying the bonds of undying friendship.

Mistletoe

◆———◆———◆

Mother of pearls

In Norse mythology, the god Baldur was killed by a spear made of mistletoe despite the goddess Frigga having made every other living thing swear not to harm him. Mistletoe had been overlooked by Frigga, even though it had the power to kill a god.

Living high up on host trees such as oak or apple, mistletoe is largely unnoticed for most of the year, but its pearl-like berries, produced in winter, are prized for their mystical powers. To preserve mistletoe's potency, some people avoided letting it touch the ground during harvesting. The Gaul druids particularly revered mistletoe that grew on oak, which was considered a sacred tree, and their priests would cut it with a golden sickle, catching the pieces in a white shawl. The sprigs were then hung over doorways as a defence against storms.

In ancient Rome, women were said to carry mistletoe to protect their fertility, and in Austria mistletoe was hidden in the bedrooms of couples trying to conceive. The Ainu people of Japan improved the fertility of their soil by cutting mistletoe leaves into tiny pieces, blessing them, and then mixing them with seed before sowing. Kissing under mistletoe brought indoors at Christmas is a British tradition that was taken to the US (where the similar genus *Phoradendron* is used).

Heather

❖

The lucky flower

A plant of heaths and moorland found across Europe and the Mediterranean, the common heather (*Calluna vulgaris*) can survive where little else grows. It is an iconic plant of the Scottish Highlands, where it is known as "ling". In Scottish folklore, a patch of white heather marks the final resting place of fairies or the ground where no blood has been shed in battle.

A sprig of white heather, a symbol of protection and good luck, is included in a Scottish bride's bouquet and in a groom's buttonhole, a custom derived from a Gaelic legend popularized in an 18th-century epic poem by James Macpherson. According to the story, a young man named Oscar, dying in battle, instructs his messenger to deliver a sprig of purple heather to his lover Malvina as a symbol of his love. As she weeps in grief, her tears fall upon the heather and turn its flowers white. Malvina then declares: "May the white heather, symbol of my sorrow, bring good fortune to all who find it."

Heather is a tough twiggy plant with many uses. It is a durable thatching material and also a dye plant. The aroma from the dried flowers is thought to promote sleep, so heather-stuffed mattresses were once popular. A "moorland tea" of the flowering shoots was used to treat coughs, colds, and urinary tract infections, and to soothe nerves. In Austria, heather tea is a traditional drink for treating kidney and bladder problems.

Ericas, which are related to heathers, but with needle-like leaves, are a more diverse group of plants, growing from the semi-alpine regions of northern Italy to the South African fynbos. The tree heath (*E. arborea*) from the Mediterranean and North Africa, is used in traditional medicine. In Turkey and Algeria, it is made into a health-giving tea.

Hellebore

❖

The Christmas rose

In European folklore, the origin of the Christmas rose (*Helleborus niger*) is explained by a tale in which a poor shepherd sets out for Bethlehem to pay homage to the newborn Jesus. Bitterly cold, and unable to find any flowers to pick as a gift, he breaks down in despair. As his tears touch the ground, white flowers appear in their place. Full of joy, he gathers them up as his gift, hence the name "Christmas rose".

An old German name for the Christmas rose is *nieswurz*, meaning "sneezewort", as a fine powder of the dried plants caused sneezing, which would see off evil spirits and disease. In medieval times, the flower was planted near the doors of houses to protect their occupants from evil spirits. The flowers are also known as "oracle roses", as according to German folklore, if you put twelve flower buds in a glass of water before Christmas you can predict the weather for the year ahead. Each flower bud represents one month, and if the bud opens by Christmas Eve then good weather is predicted for that particular month.

All parts of all hellebores are toxic. The ancient Greeks warned against it, although they used *H. niger* as a cure for mental instability, hence the 19th-century meaning for the species – "relieve my anxiety".

Azalea

◈

The cuckoo's calling card

Blooming Azalea in Blue Pot (c.1920) by Ohara Koson

" Once grown on hills, now blooming
in gardens ... send a message to God
and let azalea be the king of flowers. "

Bai Juyi (772–846)

The original parent of the winter-flowering azalea is the tender *Rhododendron simsii*. Native to south China, where it grows wild on the hillsides of the Yangtze valley, its red flowers light up the landscape in spring. In China, the azalea has several names: *yingshanhong*, meaning "reflect mountain red", and *dujuan*, which means "cuckoo", because the plant flowers when the cuckoo calls in spring.

Chinese legend has it that the red azalea sprang from blood spat out by the constantly calling cuckoo. In another version of the story, the cuckoo sang until it spat blood, and this stained the azalea red and hastened spring. The *dujuan* was a popular subject in ninth-century Chinese poetry, in particular that of the former government official Bai Juyi, who went to live in a Buddhist monastery, wrote poetry, and grew plants. Azaleas also feature in Chinese art of the period.

The Chinese initially cultivated azaleas in containers and displayed them only when they were in bloom, which coincided with Chinese New Year. When the British plant hunter Robert Fortune visited Chinese nurseries in 1852, he found cultivars of *R. simsii* that sported white flowers with red or purple stripes and sent them back to Britain.

In the late 19th century, Belgian and Dutch nurseries would sell their own selections of azaleas with double flowers in shades of pink, red, and white as indoor winter pot plants. Today, the name Ghent azaleas denotes those grown in east Flanders. In milder climates, such as the southern states of the US, cultivars of *R. simsii*, known as Formosa azaleas, are sold as spring-flowering garden shrubs.

The Victorian flower meaning for azalea is "temperance", which is said to refer to their ability to take only what they need from poor, dry soil.

Orange Blossom

The scent of sunshine

Orange trees are associated with generosity. Each tree is long-lived and offers fragrant blossom, slow-ripening fruit, and evergreen foliage. Humans have been cultivating these tough trees for well over 2,000 years. The writings of the Chinese statesman Yan Ying, in the sixth century BCE, refers to oranges and mentions the etiquette of peeling them at court.

Both the bitter and the sweet orange are hybrids of *Citrus x aurantium* from tropical and semi-tropical southeast Asia and southern China. A 12th-century book about oranges, *Ju Lu*, by Han Yanzhi, describes the cultivation of 28 types of citrus, including mandarin (*C. reticulata*), the favourite for eating; sweet orange; and bitter orange, desired for its fragrant rind. All were, and still are, grown as potted plants in China and sold as New Year gifts to wish the recipients prosperity and good fortune.

In the first century CE, the bitter orange found its way to Rome, where it was cultivated. In the ninth century, the Arabs took it to the Middle East and later to southern Spain. A tragic love story set in the emirate of Granada at the time of the Nasrid dynasty (1230–1492) tells how the fragrance of orange blossom was first captured. According to the story, a powerful sultan was in love with a beautiful girl and commissioned a young architect to build new rooms for their coming nuptials. However, the girl fell for the architect, whom she met secretly at night in the garden. As the couple lay on a rug under the trees, the aroma of orange blossom in the air mingled with the scent of their

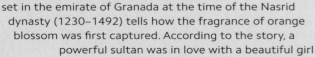

> **"** Here orange trees with blossoms and pendants shine And vernal honours to their autumn join. **"**

Alexander Pope, 18th century

Sunset in Liguria by Gaetano Previati (1852–1920)

" Youths and enamoured
maidens vie to wear
This flower, their bosoms grace,
or curled amid their hair. "

Catullus (c. 84–54 BCE)

The Bride (c. 1907) by Gari Melchers

bodies. In the morning, the fragrance of orange blossom was detected in the rug and the secret was out. In his fury, the sultan killed his fiancée and scattered her ashes. To his despair, the aroma of the lovers remained in the air, as the scent of orange blossom often does today. When a fresh breeze blows through the Alhambra's gardens, the city of Granada is filled with its penetrating and unforgettable fragrance.

The bitter orange reached the Americas and the Caribbean in the late 15th century. It later naturalized in tropical and semi-tropical areas. In Brazil, infusions were made from the dried flowers to treat colds, and in Nicaragua a decoction of dried root, fruit, and leaf is taken to treat various health problems, including fever, hypertension, and diarrhoea.

In 19th century floriography, the orange blossom's white petals represented chastity and it was associated with bridal festivities. Elizabeth Wirt's *Flora's Dictionary* (1829) says that orange blossom conveyed the message "your purity equals your loveliness", a compliment to the bride. Queen Victoria's choice of an orange blossom headdress to hold her veil in place at her wedding in 1840 ensured that orange blossom became a feature of British weddings for many decades. As real orange blossom was in short supply, wax wreaths or fabric flowers that imitated orange blossom were sometimes used instead, and had the advantage of becoming treasured keepsakes. Orange blossom was also worn or carried by bridesmaids, as a symbol of what their future held.

Bridal flowers

In the Middle Ages, a bridal bouquet of fragrant flowers and spices was a practical way to mask the odour of unwashed bodies. Parts of bouquets were often eaten after the ceremony, as it was believed they would help the bride conceive. In later centuries, the flowers chosen for a bouquet had symbolic significance. Lily of the valley symbolized a bride's virginity, jasmine represented hopes of wedded bliss, and myrtle or peonies were to ensure a long marriage.

Euphorbia pulcherrima from *The Botanist* (1836)

Poinsettia

The flame flower

In the wild, *Euphorbia pulcherrima* is native to Mexico and Guatemala. In December, as the nights in these countries lengthen, its bracts (leaves around its tiny gold flowers) turn from green to crimson. This happens at the time of the winter solstice, so the Aztecs called it *cuetlaxochitl* – "mortal flower that perishes and withers like all that is pure" – to symbolize the new life earned by warriors who had died in battle and were said to return as hummingbirds.

In Mexico, there is a story about a girl on her way to church on Christmas Eve without an offering for the altar. As she walked, an angel appeared and suggested she pick weeds. When she offered her gift, the weeds burst into red blooms – the poinsettia. From then on, it is said, they were known as *flor de la noche buena* (flower of the good night).

When Joel Roberts Poinsett was the US ambassador to Mexico in 1825–29, he noticed that *flor de la noche buena* was used to adorn churches at Christmas time. He called it the "Mexican flame flower", and took samples back to South Carolina. A century later, "Poinsettia", named after him, became the festive pot plants we know today.

Amaryllis

A majestic bloom

The large bulbs of the amaryllis send up one or two tall stems topped by spectacular star-shaped flowers. They were popular indoor plants in European and American drawing-rooms in the 19th century, despite supposedly representing pride because of the splendour of their flowers.

In 1821, these South American plants were given their own genus, *Hippeastrum*, but are still incorrectly known as amaryllis (the genus name of a South African species). The name *Hippeastrum*, from the Greek *hippeus*, meaning mounted knight, was chosen because the bracts (petal-like leaves) appear to stand up like the ears of horses as the buds open.

More than 600 hybrids have been bred in Europe and the US as ornamental plants, often sold around Christmas and the New Year, but the original South American plants – tropical or semi-tropical species found in Brazil, Bolivia, and Peru – have played an important role in traditional medicine, even though many of them are toxic. One of these is *H. puniceum*, which is widely used to breed hybrids. The Siona and Secoya people of eastern Ecuador have traditionally grown it in their gardens, and used the bulb, crushed in water and then roasted or boiled, as a purgative for stomach ache.

Tropical Orchid

Fascinating beauty

Orchids are one of the most diverse groups of flowering plants, with gorgeous blooms, and in some cases, beautiful scents. Vanilla comes from the fermented pods that hang down from the vine-like orchid *Vanilla planifolia*. Although it is now mainly grown in Madagascar, the orchid's original home is Central America.

In eastern Mexico, this orchid is still grown and appreciated in Veracruz, just as it once was by the Aztecs, who knew it as *tlilxóchitl* – the black orchid – because its long pods turned black

" There is an orchid as beautiful
as the seven deadly sins. **"**

Oscar Wilde, *A Woman of No Importance*, 1893

when they dried out. The
Spanish learned of vanilla from
the Aztecs, who regarded it as
both a precious medicine and,
when mixed with chocolate,
a powerful aphrodisiac.

Before the rise of the Aztecs,
the Totonac people told how vanilla
was born from the blood of a princess.
According to their legend, King Teniztli
had a beautiful daughter and named her
Tzacopontziza (Morning Star). To keep
her pure and away from mortal men,
the king had Tzacopontziza dedicated
to the service of Tonacayahua, the
goddess of fertility. But when a
handsome young man named Zkata Oxga
(Running Deer) saw her going about her
temple duties, the pair fell in love.

Although the couple tried to escape
to the mountains together, the high priests
of the temple captured them and cut off their
heads, throwing their bodies into a mountain
ravine. When the blood of the lovers seeped into
the ground, a bush sprang up entwined by a beautiful
orchid vine. After its flowers had finished blooming, long
pods hung down. As these dried and darkened, they emitted
an exquisite perfume more beautiful than anything the Totonac
people had ever known. They believed that the divine scent
was the pure, sweet soul of their Princess Tzacopontziza and
declared the orchid sacred.

The most familiar tropical orchid is the moth orchid
(*Phalaenopsis*), originally from Asia. In the Philippines, these orchids
are known as *mariposa* – Spanish for butterfly– because their flat
flowers, arranged on long stems above the leaves, look like butterflies
in flight. Much loved for their beauty and their wide range of colours,
they are often given as gifts. In 1836, the first *Phalenopsis aphrodite*

to be brought to Britain was offered to the Duke of Devonshire. He paid 100 guineas for the specimen and then sent his plant hunters off to Asia to hunt for more species.

It is Asia's *Dendrobium* orchids, whose leaves and flowers grow up the length of chunky stems, that have the richest history of herbal use and symbolism. In the wild, *Dendrobium nobile* grows in deciduous forests in the Himalayan foothills, as well as rocky areas of Myanmar, Thailand, and Vietnam. In traditional Chinese medicine, it is known as *shihu* – rock living – and a plant that can grow in such places is considered strong, with fortifying properties. Stems are

> **"** If you are in the company of good people, it is like entering a room full of orchids. **"**

Confucius (551–479 BCE)

Eighteenth-century Japanese screen depicting orchids

cut before flowering and dried, then used as a tea, as a general tonic for long life, or to nourish and stimulate the stomach and lungs. *Dendrobium* orchids were once grown by Japanese royalty for their beautiful shape and fragrant flowers, so they are still considered noble plants and are often given as a present, conferring peace and good fortune.

In China, the most esteemed orchids are the *Cymbidium* orchids. Their green-yellow or green-brown flowers may seem modest compared to the spectacular colours of other tropical orchids, but in China the whole plant is admired for its combination of scent, flowers, and graceful foliage. The ancient Chinese philosopher Confucius (551–479 BCE) praised *Cymbidium* orchids because they grew in inaccessible gorges yet gave off their fragrance regardless of the absence of admirers. He compared this quality to a person with integrity upholding their virtues even in difficult circumstances.

During the Song dynasty (960–1279CE), growing a wide range of orchids became a popular hobby for retired scholars and officials, who also made them the subject of paintings, wood block printing, and poetry. The scent of *Cymbidium* orchids is considered the "ancestor of all fragrances", and so potted plants or a painting of this orchid are symbols of friendship and often given as gifts. Rare species of wild *Cymbidium* orchids are very valuable, with one specimen fetching some 4.6 million yuan (more than £500,000) in 2005, when prices were at their height.

Orchid garlands

In Thailand, garlands known as *phuang malai* have been popular offerings since the early days of the Rattanakosin Kingdom (1782–1932), and girls in the palace were expected to acquire the skills to make them. Orchid flowers form surprisingly sturdy and long-lasting garlands. There are three types: *malai chai diao* to show respect; *malai song chai* for a wedding couple; and *malai chamruai*, which are given as good luck souvenirs at parties.

Aloe Vera

Arabia's healer

Known to humans for several thousand years, the aloe has acquired many meanings, ranging from protection and good luck to bitterness and grief, but it is probably most famous for the healing properties of its leaves. These contain yellow liquid and a clear gel-like substance: the liquid was used in the past for digestive problems and is responsible for the plant's bitter taste; the gel provides a soothing remedy for skin problems such as burns, including sunburn, insect bites, and wounds.

The aloe plant originated in the Arabian peninsula, its name said to derive from the Arabic word *alloeh*, meaning "shining and bitter substance". The ancient Egyptians knew it as the "plant of immortality" because it can survive for long periods without soil or water, and because it was also used as an ingredient in the embalming process. It is also said that Cleopatra used aloe plants to keep her skin looking youthful. According to the Roman author Pliny the Elder, Aristotle persuaded Alexander the Great to capture Socotra Island in the Indian Ocean, famous for aloes, to provide a source of the plant for treating the wounds of Roman soldiers. The aloe is still sometimes known as the "burn plant" or "first-aid plant" and its gel is included in a range of medicinal and cosmetic products.

The aloe also has symbolic value. In the Islamic faith, it is traditionally a token of good luck. Pilgrims returning from Mecca would sometimes hang aloe over their doors to protect the household from evil. In Victorian England, on the other hand, the plant came to mean acute sorrow, bitterness, and grief, based on its bitter taste.

Illustration of *Aloe vera*, from *Phytographia curiosa*, published in 1702

❝ The aloe is made the emblem of acute sorrow, on account of its painful bitterness. ❞

Henry Phillips, 1831

Viburnum

Bitter beauty

Viburnum (*Viburnum opulus*) grows across northern Europe, Scandinavia, Canada, and the US. Also known as the Guelder rose, after a region of the Netherlands where the "snowball" viburnum was cultivated, viburnum is loved for its clouds of white or pink-tinged flowers in summer and glossy red berries in autumn. In Ukraine, where it is called *kalyna*, the plant has a rich folk history, celebrated in art, poetry, stories, embroidery, and songs. Bunches of *kalyna* were once hung in doorways to ward off evil spirits, and it is common to see *kalyna* bushes planted in gardens as well as growing in the wild, because the plant is a potent symbol of home. In Canada, Kalyna County, in Alberta, is the heartland of Ukrainian culture in the country. It was settled by Ukrainians who emigrated to Canada in the late 19th century.

Widely associated with both virginity and fertility, *kalyna* features in many Ukrainian wedding songs: the red juice of its berries symbolizes blood, and the expression "breaking the kalyna" is a euphemism for a bride losing her virginity; references to a "bridge of *kalyna* branches" refer to the transition from single to married life and also alludes to everything in life that will never come again. For this reason, *kalyna* is also associated with the death of a true love, especially of soldiers who have died in battle. Women would promise to plant a *kalyna* bush on the graves of their soldier husbands should

Guelder Rose – Snowball, from *The Language of Fairies and Plants* (c 1910)

> " My love for you is filled to the brim
> with the bitterness of the kalyna. "

Liubov Zabashta

they die. According to Ukrainian folklore, birds would bring the dead news of their loved ones when they came to feed on the berries in autumn.

Ukrainians and other Slavic people harvest viburnum berries to make jams and jellies, and for use in traditional remedies. Picked after the first frosts when they are less tart, the berries are stewed to make a distinctive-smelling bitter tea that is then sweetened with honey to soothe coughs and applied to the skin to help cure acne and other skin complaints; a tincture made from the bark of the tree, which must be collected in spring before the leaves appear, is thought to be effective against all kinds of cramp.

Bird-of-paradise Flower

❦

South African icon

This exotic-looking plant with bunches of alternating blue and orange flowers is a native of South Africa and KwaZulu-Natal. It arrived at London's Kew Gardens in 1773, and was given the scientific name *Strelitzia reginae* in honour of Charlotte of Mecklenburg-Streltiz, wife of the British monarch, George III. The plant was introduced into California in the mid-19th century, and in 1952 it was named the official flower of the city of Los Angeles.

At some point, *Strelitzia* acquired its popular name from the flower's striking resemblance to the tropical bird of paradise in flight – the upright petals suggest the bird's raised wings and the sheath from which they emerge resembles the bird's tail streaming out behind. From some angles, clusters of flowers can look like a group of brightly coloured birds. The bird-of-paradise is sometimes known as the crane flower because it resembles that bird's long neck and beak.

The flower has come to symbolize freedom and optimism. It also represents magnificence and splendour due to its royal connection. Because of its great height – plants can reach up to

2 m (6 ft) tall – it often stands out from the crowd, so it also represents individuality. It can also symbolize paradise on earth and an aspiration to higher things.

In 1994, the Kirstenbosch National Botanical Gardens in South Africa released a cultivar of *Strelitzia reginae* with golden-yellow and blue flowers. It took 20 years to create and was initially known as Kirstenbosch Gold. Two years later, following a visit to the gardens by Nelson Mandela, it was renamed Mandela's Gold in his honour.

" Nothing says South African flora more than *Strelitzia reginae.* "

Nick Bailey, 2018

Anthurium

+———•———+

Straight from the heart

Botanical illustration of Anthurium, 1886

In the 1850s, a young Austrian naturalist, Karl Scherzer – later ennobled as Karl Ritter von Scherzer – was exploring the jungles and rainforests of Central and South America when he was struck by a plant of extraordinary beauty with what appeared to be huge heart-shaped flowers. He took the plant back to Europe, where it was later named after him: *Anthurium scherzerianum*.

Since Scherzer's time, more than 1,000 species of anthurium have been identified, although there is only one other red variety – *A. andraeanum* from Colombia and Ecuador. It is also one of the most widely cultivated species and has become a popular houseplant in many parts of the world.

> **" The heart-shaped houseplant's waxy leaves curve inward like an invitation. "**
>
> **Bonnie Wertheim**, *New York Times*, 2017

Anthurium is commonly known as the flamingo flower, though what we may think of as its flower is not a flower at all. The brightly coloured growth is a modified leaf, known as a spathe. The actual flowers are tiny – hundreds of them cluster in the pale spike, called a spadix, that sticks out from the spathe. In nature, the brilliant hues of the spathe attract insects to pollinate the plant.

The heart-shaped spathe and phallic spadix have associated anthurium with love and sex. Its easy adaptability and the cheerful red spathe also suggest home and hospitality. Research by the US space agency, NASA, has shown that anthuriums are good air purifiers – in confined indoor spaces, they help to remove ammonia and other potentially harmful chemicals from the air.

Gardenia

— ◊ —

Symbol of refinement

Gardenia, 18th-century watercolour

The gardenia's headily scented white flowers, set off against dark, glossy, evergreen leaves, have conjured up many symbolic associations over the centuries, including refinement, elegance, purity, and feminine strength. In Victorian times, it became an item of male adornment, too. Well-dressed men liked to wear gardenia buttonholes when out and about in fashionable city haunts. They are still popular at weddings, especially for the groom and groomsmen.

" Finally, there was just peace like the sweetness of gardenias. "

Wallace Stevens

Related to the coffee plant, the gardenia is native to the forests and mountains of southeast Asia. The Chinese valued it for both its beauty and its medicinal value, and they were cultivating it by around the 10th century CE. Gardenias featured in Chinese paintings and other art forms from the time of the Song Dynasty (960–1279). Called *zhi zi*, it established itself as an ingredient in traditional Chinese medicine. A tincture made from its fruit is believed to clear heat in the body and was used to treat irritability and insomnia along with fevers and pancreatitis. The flower petals are used to scent tea.

In the 18th century, Dutch traders cultivated the plant in their Cape of Good Hope colony in southern Africa. From there, specimens were taken to Europe. By the 1760s, Scottish-born naturalist Alexander Garden was growing the flower in Charleston, South Carolina. This is where the plant's Latin name (*Gardenia jasminoides*) originated.

Flowering Quince

Precious fruit

“ She threw a quince to me;
In requital I gave a bright gem.
Meaning I would love her forever. ”

The Book of Songs, 600 BCE

Flowering quinces (*Chaenomeles*) are easily coaxed into flowering in winter if their stems are cut and brought indoors. The twiggy branches studded with red, pink, or white flowers lend themselves to *ikebana* – Japanese flower arranging. As its name suggests, the wild species of *C. japonica* is originally from Japan and Korea, while *C. speciosa* (now *C. lagenaria*) is native all over China.

The name quince was first used to describe the fragrant yellow fruit of the related *Cydonia oblonga*, in *The Books of Songs* (600 BCE), the oldest collection of Chinese poetry. In one poem, a playful exchange of gifts between two young people tests their suitability for marriage. A young woman throws a quince that she has plucked from her family's garden, while her lover throws her a precious gem – meaning that she means everything to him.

The fruit of *C. speciosa* has been used in traditional Chinese medicine since the fifth century, and was described in the *Mingyi Bielu* (*Additional Records of Famous Physicians*) by the Taoist pharmacologist Tao Hongjing (456–536 CE). Harvested in autumn, the fruit is either dried for use in decoctions or consumed fresh. One of its properties is that it relaxes the tendons and muscles, so it is often used in association with peony to relieve cramp in the abdomen and lower limbs.

The quince tree has flourished in the Mediterranean since the time of the ancient Greeks. Its fruit was dedicated to Aphrodite, goddess of love, and so it became a symbol of beauty, fertility, and a happy marriage. In Greek mythology, the golden apples given to the goddess Hera on her wedding day and guarded by the Hesperides, three goddess-nymphs, are thought to be quinces, as apples were not golden-coloured in ancient times. The nymphs and the precious fruit were regarded as the golden orange light of sunset, which was believed to be a celebration of the union of Hera and the god Zeus.

Index

Acknowledgments

Toucan Books

Editorial Director Ellen Dupont; **Editor** Dorothy Stannard; **Designer** Dave Jones; **Picture Researcher** Sharon Southren; **Authenticity Reader** Kit Heyam; **Proofreader** Julie Brooke; **Indexer** Marie Lorimer

Additional Writers Helen Douglas-Cooper; Andrew Kerr-Jarrett

Picture Credits

The publisher would like to thank the following for their kind permission to reproduce their photographs:

11 Dreamstime.com: Oleksandr Kostiuchenko. **13 Alamy Stock Photo:** The Natural History Museum. **15 Bridgeman Images. 18 Bridgeman Images:** Photo © Christie's Images. **19 Dreamstime.com:** Elena Elisseeva. **23 Wellcome Collection. 25 Los Angeles County Museum of Art. 26 The Walters Art Museum, Baltimore:** Acquired by Henry Walters. **32 Dorling Kindersley:** Neil Fletcher. **34 Rijksmuseum, Amsterdam. 35 Alamy Stock Photo:** MehmetO. **39 Alamy Stock Photo:** Pictures Now. **40 akg-images:** arkivi. **42 The Cleveland Museum Of Art:** Gift of The Print Club of Cleveland in memory of William J. Eastman. **43 Dreamstime.com:** Alfio Scisetti. **53 Minneapolis Institute of Art:** The John R. Van Derlip Fund; purchase from the collection of Elizabeth and Willard Clark. **58 Alamy Stock Photo:** mauritius images GmbH. **59 Alamy Stock Photo:** Heritage Image Partnership Ltd. **60 Bridgeman Images:** Accademia Italiana, London. **62 Dreamstime.com:** Settapong Dee-ud. **63 The Cleveland Museum Of Art:** Edward L. Whittemore Fund. **64 Getty Images:** Josh Westrich / Corbis. **67 Mary Evans Picture Library. 69 Dreamstime.com:** Beldesigne. **70 Dreamstime. com:** Wasana Jaigunta. **71 Getty Images:** Heritage Images / Contributor / Hulton Fine Art Collection. **72 Shutterstock. com:** PRISMA ARCHIVO. **75 The Art Institute of Chicago:** Frederick W. Gookin Collection. **76 Alamy Stock Photo:** GRANGER - Historical Picture Archive. **78 Dreamstime.com:** Photowitch. **80 Dreamstime.com:** Henadzi Pechan. **81 Getty Images:** Heritage Images / Contributor. **83 Dreamstime.com:** Ncl. **85 Alamy Stock Photo:** The Print Collector. **87 Dreamstime.com:** Pmakin. **89 Getty Images:** sarayut Thaneerat / Moment. **91 The Art Institute of Chicago:** Mr. and Mrs. Martin A. Ryerson Collection. **93 Alamy Stock Photo:** Hamza Khan. **95 Dorling Kindersley:** Gary Ombler: Green and Gorgeous Flowers. **96 Dreamstime.com:** Pavel Parmenov. **99 Bridgeman Images:** The Stapleton Collection. **100 Dreamstime. com:** Lcrms7. **102 Alamy Stock Photo:** Album. **103 Dreamstime.com:** Marc Bruxelle. **104 Dreamstime. com:** Chernetskaya. **105 Dreamstime.com:** Andrii Bielikov. **107 Shutterstock.com:** Losmandarinas. **108 Alamy Stock Photo:** Pictures Now. **111 Dreamstime.com:** Alfio Scisetti. **113 SuperStock:** FLO / Science and Society. **117 Alamy Stock Photo:** Album. **118 Alamy Stock Photo:** Peter Barritt. **121 Bridgeman Images:** © The Wilson. **122 Alamy Stock Photo:** ART Collection. **125 Mary Evans Picture Library:** The Pictures Now Image Collection. **130 The Cleveland Museum Of Art:** Bequest of Leonard C. Hanna, Jr. **131 Getty Images:** Jethuynh / Moment Open. **133 Alamy Stock Photo:** The Picture Art Collection. **134 The Cleveland Museum Of Art:** Gift of The Print Club of Cleveland in honor of Mrs. William G. Mather. **135 Alamy Stock Photo:** Alfio Scisetti. **136 Alamy Stock Photo:** 916 collection. **137 Dreamstime.com:** Richard Griffin. **139 Alamy Stock Photo:** PRISMA ARCHIVO. **140 Alamy Stock Photo:** Artepics. **142 SuperStock:** Album / Florilegius / Album Archivo. **146 Dreamstime.com:** Pindiyath100. **149 Alamy Stock Photo:** MNS Photo. **151 Mary Evans Picture Library:** Florilegius. **157 Alamy Stock Photo:** SuperStock. **159 Alamy Stock Photo:** thislife pictures. **163 Dreamstime.com:** Alfio Scisetti. **164 Rijksmuseum, Amsterdam:** Gift of J. Perrée, Eindhoven. **166 Getty Images:** iStock/ photomaru. **167 Bridgeman Images:** Alinari Archives, Florence. **168 Smithsonian American Art Museum:** Gift of John Gellatly. **170 Alamy Stock Photo:** Florilegius. **173 Dreamstime.com:** Jiri Hera / Jirkaejc. **174 Alamy Stock Photo:** Heritage Image Partnership Ltd. **177 Bridgeman Images:** The Stapleton Collection. **178 Getty Images:** Westend61 / Getty Images Plus. **179 Mary Evans Picture Library:** Peter & Dawn Cope Collection. **182 Mary Evans Picture Library:** Florilegius. **184 Bridgeman Images:** Natural History Museum, London. **185 Getty Images:** juicybits / iStock. **187 Dreamstime.com:** Elengrant.

All other images © Dorling Kindersley